Recovery From Narcissistic Abuse Workbook

Daily Rituals, Visualizations, and Affirmations to Heal the Mind, Body, and Soul

Harmony Fielding

Table of Contents

Introduction

You do have a story; it lies articulate and waiting to be written behind your silence and your suffering. –Anne Rice

If there's anything I have learned from my own journey of healing and growth, it's that the path to healing is hardly a straight one. Sometimes, healing is about reflection—becoming aware of our own thoughts, emotions, and behavioral patterns. Other times, healing occurs when we get support and validation on our journey. No matter what we're recovering from and how long the process takes, healing cannot begin unless we acknowledge our need for it. This can be trickier than it sounds. When we leave behind a situation that is toxic or abusive, life becomes all about survival for a while. When all you can do is keep your head above the water, healing can take a backseat.

Not only that, but one of the main characteristics of narcissistic (and other forms of) abuse is that it breaks us down and makes us doubt our own selves. What this means is that even after physically detaching ourselves from our abusive partner, we might not be able to trust our own instincts and needs for a long time. Now, if you have kids with your narcissistic ex and need to co-parent with them, the entire process becomes even more challenging.

I've had firsthand experience of this as a mom of two who separated from her narcissistic partner of 10 years, and I can tell you that it took me a while to give myself the tools, space, and kindness needed to completely heal from the situation. In my previous book, Empowered Co-Parenting With A Narcissistic-Ex, I talked about "cutting the ties," detaching from the emotional turmoil, and setting boundaries with my ex while protecting my own peace and my children's well-being at all times. This book serves as a companion to my previous book, with its focus on inner work, chakra healing, and spirituality.

If you're someone who is separated or divorced from your narcissistic partner, you will need a sense of closure to emotionally detach yourself from your ex and your past. Not only that, but you will need to acknowledge the pain and confusion you've been experiencing to truly heal and move on from the relationship. When I finally left my partner, I was traumatized and extremely unsure of who I was. Even as the relationship had come to an end, I was still plagued with stress, uncertainty, and intrusive thoughts. When I finally decided that enough was enough, I started implementing the practices that we'll be discussing in this book. Slowly but surely, I found myself healing and moving on from my ex. Two years on, I feel free and empowered on my journey, and I want to help others who might be struggling with theirs.

If you've picked up this book, chances are, you are dealing with one or more of the following questions on your journey:

- How do I decenter the narcissist from my life?
- How do I prevent flashbacks and intrusive thoughts, and how do I stop feeling attacked on a psychic level?
- How do I truly let go and move on from the narcissist and their effect on me?
- How do I stop feeling stressed and anxious all the time?
- What can I do to overcome constant negativity and finally achieve a positive mindset?
- How do I regain my sense of inner calm and come back into balance with my true self?
- How do I regain my sense of spontaneity and inventiveness, take risks without jeopardizing my family, and grow as a person?
- How do I ensure that I don't repeat the patterns that led me to attract a narcissist in my life? How do I make better choices for myself and my children in the future?
- How do I have faith in myself and feel more empowered on this journey?

This last question is especially important because many of us take time to regain our sense of control and empowerment after leaving a toxic relationship. Through this book, I hope you can finally script your own narrative. Before we move on to the exercises mentioned in each chapter, let's take an emotional and spiritual inventory of ourselves. Let's also briefly understand what chakras are and how chakra healing can be a powerful tool in helping us recover from narcissistic abuse.

Before we move ahead, I would like you to reflect deeply and write down the answers to the following questions:

- How do I feel right now? What are some of the most significant emotions I'm going through?
- What are some of the fears and insecurities I deal with on an everyday basis?
- What does my physical and mental health look like currently?
- What are some of the blocks I face when it comes to expressing myself on a regular basis?
- How do I view myself currently, and is there something I would like to improve with respect to my self-esteem?
- Do I believe that I have the ability to take control of my life?
- Am I capable of loving and trusting myself and others?
- Do I feel like I'm living a life that is aligned with my truest self?
- Do I feel connected or detached from those around me?

Remember, there are no right or wrong answers to any of these questions. Neither can these questions be answered in a line or two. You will need to sit with these questions and reflect on whatever emotions come up during the process. Also, these questions can act as a basis for our understanding of chakras.

To understand chakras, we need to understand the presence of a "subtle" body. While our physical body is what we see, our subtle body is our energetic self. In this energetic body lie chakras—literally translated as "wheels"—through which the life force energy flows (known as prana, chi, or qi). This prana is essential in maintaining physical, mental, emotional, and spiritual balance in our body. When our chakras are out of balance, it can lead to a whole host of problems for us. In order to align them, we need to do a lot of inner work, yoga, and meditation—among other spiritual practices.

While there are different chakra systems recognized in the ancient practices of Hinduism and Buddhism, we will be working with the seven chakra systems for this book. As we move from the first to the seventh chakra, we'll learn to progressively heal aspects of ourselves. In each chapter, we'll first understand how our chakra might be out of balance due to the abuse that we're recovering from. Then, we'll move on to exercises, rituals, and practical advice that can help us heal and balance our chakra. Also, it's important to heal our "lower" chakras before we move on to the "higher" ones—which means that this book will focus on physical and mental health as much as on spiritual health.

Before we start, I ask you to take a deep breath and give yourself grace. The journey you're on is not easy, but it is entirely worth it. You'll face challenges in your healing and spiritual journey, and some days will likely be harder than others. All I ask is that you stay committed to yourself throughout this process and have faith that you'll eventually find your way.

Chapter 1:

Rooted in Recovery— Cultivating Safety, Security, and Grounding After Narcissistic Abuse

He is a wise man who does not grieve for the things which he has not, but rejoices for those which he has. —Epictetus

To understand this quote in-depth, we first need to understand what the root chakra signifies. The root chakra—also known as the muladhara—is the lowest chakra in the subtle body. This is the chakra of stability, security, and our basic needs of nutrition, rest, and balance. When this chakra is aligned, we feel safe, fearless, and grounded. When this is not the case, we might be plagued with both physical and mental health problems. On the physical front, we might have trouble getting adequate rest and eating nutritious food. This might lead to weakness and lack of proper balance in the long run.

When it comes to mental health, imagine how you feel when you're anxious, stressed, or out of balance with yourself. Think of the root chakra as the base for everything. If the foundation is strong, your mind will be focused on building other aspects of your life. However, if the base is weak or unstable, all your energy will go into making yourself feel safe. As people who have been victims of narcissistic abuse, we often find ourselves shaken to the core. Sometimes, we struggle to understand what is real and stable in our lives, even after we've moved away from the relationship itself. If you find yourself plagued with fear, your root chakra might be in need of healing. Here are a few questions that can help you understand whether your root chakra is out of balance:

- Do I feel like I'm on autopilot when it comes to work, relationships, and life?
- Do I feel a sense of security and stability in my own life?
- Do I deal with change in a negative manner—often worrying how it would impact my mental health?
- Do I frequently find myself rooted in the past or worried about the future—so much so that it derails my everyday life?
- Do I feel aggressive because of a lack of control over my life?
- Do I find it difficult to come back to a state of balance after a triggering episode?
- Am I able to maintain a healthy diet as well as a regular exercise and sleeping regimen?
- Do I find manifestations effective in my life?

Am I able to maintain boundaries in my life and be assertive when needed?

Make a note of the number of questions that you've answered yes to and those you have said no to. If more than half of these questions have been answered as "yes," your root chakra might be seriously out of alignment. Now, think about why you currently feel so unstable and unsure in your life. One of the major reasons why this happens is that abuse and trauma can often make us lose the ability to feel empowered in the present moment. At any given time, we find ourselves focused on the things we've lost and those that are absent from our lives. While this is a very natural response to trauma, it keeps us from embracing life fully. This is why the quote asks us to focus on what we have in our lives, to accept what we don't have or what we're struggling with, and not to let absence and loss overpower our narrative.

Before we move on to the various practices that can help us align our root chakra, let's look at a case study to help understand this scenario better.

Rebuilding Trust and Stability

Anyone who knew Maria saw her as a strong and grounded person. She was always sure of herself as well as her needs. It took a lot to unsettle her, and she prided herself on the fact that she could handle anything that life threw at her. However, all this drastically changed when Dan came into her life. It took Maria a while to realize that Dan was a narcissist who was insidiously affecting her physical, mental, and emotional health through his abusive behaviors. For a long time, she tried to simply focus on herself and not let Dan drain her energy, but she soon realized that it wasn't worth it. When she finally decided to break off her relationship with Dan, she expected to also regain her strength and stability.

This, however, proved to be more difficult than she had anticipated. She realized that she had been neglecting her physical and mental health for a long time because of the challenges she faced in her abusive relationship. Not only that, but her body had become a receptacle for all the abuse, even though she hadn't realized it then. Even though she was consciously aware of the fact that she was not in any danger from her ex, her body was yet to catch up. In fact, it was still reeling from being in near-constant fight-or-flight mode, and it would take a while for it to relax and feel safe in its surroundings.

It was when Maria became fully aware of the tension she had been carrying in her body for so long that she understood how her ex's abuse had changed her. Not only was she more anxious than before, but she had also lost touch with her own self over time. She worried too much about the future, constantly doubted her decisions, and had difficulty focusing on the present moment. She was easily triggered and had greater difficulty centering herself after a triggering episode.

What frustrated her the most was that she felt like she was losing control over her life. Maria had always lived life with intention and purpose, and it was unsettling for her to think that life was just passing her by while she tried to regain her bearings. Every aspect of her life felt like it was on autopilot, and this was not something that she would stand for. She was exhausted, but she had not given up on herself.

At this time, Maria summoned her sense of responsibility—something that had always helped her throughout her life. She realized that she needed to be more accountable for her life and that, by giving in to anxiety and negativity, she was simply giving away her power to her narcissistic ex. She understood that her ex didn't need to be physically present in her life in order to control it. Therefore, it was her responsibility to ensure that only she could dictate how her life looked at any given moment.

That was when Maria understood that she did not need to dwell on the past or even worry too much about the future as long as she could direct her energies fully to the present. By connecting deeply with herself in the present—and allowing her body to rest and heal—she was able to regain her strength, courage, and stability. She was getting less and less wary each day of the changes that might come her way because she was finally standing on solid ground. She knew it would take a while for her to rebuild her life, but this time, she wouldn't let anyone shake her core or question her reality. While it might take some time for her to trust someone else, she was now ready to rebuild her trust in herself, and she would start with her body. She would listen to the signals her body gave her and tap into the deep wisdom that came from connecting to the Earth through grounding practices. She also thanked her body for being patient with her when she neglected it.

Now that we know how narcissistic abuse can affect our root chakra, let's discuss a few rituals, meditations, and exercises that can help us heal our root chakra and bring back stability into our lives.

Root Chakra Healing

In this section, we'll be going through a few techniques and rituals that you can implement in your daily life.

Taking Care of Your Physical Self

Since the root chakra is deeply rooted in our physical reality, we can begin the healing process by taking care of our physical health. Here are a few steps you can take:

- Make sure that you're eating **healthy and whole foods** as much as possible. Whole foods are connected to the Earth and help channel the healing energy of the Earth into our bodies.
- Keep yourself hydrated and **avoid stimulating drinks**—as they interfere with your sleeping patterns and can exacerbate symptoms of anxiety.
- Don't compromise on **rest and sleep**. As much as possible, stick to a routine that allows you to get interrupted sleep during the night. This also means staying away from digital devices or anything that can unnecessarily stimulate your senses.

The Importance of Grounding Yourself

Even after leaving behind a toxic relationship, many of us have difficulty feeling stable and secure in our lives. This can sometimes manifest as panic or anxiety attacks—triggered by memories of the past, or it can show up in our relationships with others. A lack of grounding causes us to disconnect from the present moment and from its many blessings. Let's discuss a few methods that can help us ground ourselves.

Deepen Your Connection With Nature

One of the most powerful ways of grounding yourself is by spending more time in nature. If you're lucky enough to have access to green spaces like parks and forests, spend as much time as you can in those spaces. Even if you can only take a walk in your own garden, try to do it barefoot if possible. This way, you feel more connected to the Earth. A great time to do this is in the morning when the dew settles on the grass. The sensation that you get by walking on grass during that period is incomparable, and it can quickly put your mind at ease. What is important is that you anchor yourself to the present as you walk mindfully in your garden or a park.

"Forest bathing" is another activity you can engage in, especially if you have more on your hands. This is not something that can be rushed. You need to immerse yourself in this environment and pay close attention to your surroundings. You can simply breathe deeply as you take in the calm and quiet of the forest, or you can use your senses to take in the various shades of green, the different scents, and the numerous textures present before you. As long as you know it's safe, allow yourself to touch some leaves or trace your fingers over the bark of a tree. In the presence of nature, you will experience awe and be able to get out of your own head, especially when you have trouble controlling intrusive thoughts.

Simple Daily Grounding Practices

For us to feel grounded, we need to be connected to our bodies and breathe as much as possible. When we're constantly in fight-or-flight mode, our bodies start storing our trauma without us realizing it. This can manifest in many ways—most of which are subtle—for example, your breaths might become short and hurried, or you might develop tension in your muscles. People who live in an almost constant state of trauma and abuse begin to accept this state as their default, which is why we need certain practices that help us reconnect with the natural state of our body, mind, and soul.

Body Scan Meditation

A simple and effective way of getting in touch with your body is through body scan meditation. You can do this technique either sitting or lying down, but make sure that your feet are placed flat on the ground so that you can stay connected to the Earth at all times during this practice. Close your eyes and take a few deep breaths to begin this meditation. Start from your toes and slowly move up to the crown of your head. As you inhale deeply, notice how that area of your body feels. For example, as you focus on your toes, pay attention to whether your toes are tingling, tense, or relaxed. If they're relaxed, simply exhale slowly and move on to the next area in the body.

If you notice tension in any part of the body, make note of it without judgment or blame. Often, we get irritated at ourselves when we're faced with our own trauma. Instead, acknowledge that your leg or arm is sore, meaning you're probably holding something unpleasant within yourself. As you exhale slowly, allow that tension, pain, or anxiety to also move away from your being. Repeat this exercise for every part of your body until you reach the top. After that, simply take in a few more breaths while you acknowledge how calm and relaxed you feel in the moment.

Progressive Muscle Relaxation

In this exercise, we encourage our entire body to relax by targeting one muscle group at a time. To do this, you can lie down on the ground or sit with your feet firmly planted on the ground. Close your eyes and take three to five deep breaths. Then, focus on one muscle group at a time—for example, your calf muscles or upper arm muscles. As you inhale, slowly contract that muscle group and hold it in that state for 5–10 seconds—depending on your comfort level. Then, exhale deeply as you relax those muscles as quickly as you can. This way, your body will suddenly notice a lessening in tension—which will consequently lead to a reduction in your anxiety levels. Move on to the next muscle group and repeat this exercise until you've covered most or all of your body. Through this exercise, we're using the relaxation of our body to relax our mind.

Grounding Meditation

When we're feeling out of sorts, connecting our breath to our body can help immensely in grounding ourselves. A simple grounding technique is to stop whatever we're doing and take deep breaths for a few minutes. This apparently simple technique can have profound benefits for our stress and anxiety levels. So many of us have difficulty taking one long, deep breath simply because our bodies have almost always been in fight-or-flight mode.

Once you get comfortable with this, try to take it a step further. In this practice, as you close your eyes and take a deep breath inward, imagine that there are roots growing from the soles of your feet that reach deep underground. As they anchor themselves firmly to the Earth, imagine how they connect to you and give you life. As you inhale, imagine that these roots are taking in healing energy from the Earth and sending it to you. If, at the moment, you feel distress of any kind, imagine that you're giving them away to the Earth as you exhale. Do this for a few minutes and imagine yourself getting nourished by the Earth.

Grounding Through Your Senses

Our senses are very powerful in helping us establish a deep and meaningful connection with the world within and outside us. Normally, our senses are overwhelmed by the various types of information thrown at them. Through this exercise, we bring intentionality into the way we engage with the world. One of these techniques is known as the "Five Senses Technique." You can do this exercise anywhere, but make sure you're in a secure place, as you will need to focus entirely on the things you see, hear, or touch. This is something that you should keep in mind while doing any kind of meditation or visualization technique. Since your attention needs to be on an object, thought, or your breath—don't do these exercises when you're in public or when you need to stay alert for some other purpose.

This exercise can also be combined with a forest bath, as it allows you to pay attention to your senses. As you start this exercise, take a deep breath and note down any five things that you see around you. Pay special attention to them and notice their colors or any other characteristics that feel significant to you. After that, touch any four things around you. Then, notice three things you can hear in your environment, two things you can smell, and one thing you can taste. You can do this exercise in various combinations and permutations— such as noting five things you hear, four things you see, and so on. Also, it might not always be possible or feasible for you to touch or taste things around you. You might even consider doing this exercise as a complete visualization, meaning that you imagine seeing, tasting, hearing, smelling, and touching various things—preferably those that bring you peace and joy. In the beginning, it might be difficult to imagine these things, but you'll get better with practice. What's important is that you focus on the emotions that come up as you do this exercise.

You can also use your favorite objects to help ground you in stressful situations. For example, do you have a favorite soft toy from your childhood that makes you feel warm and safe? Are there any specific fabrics that you like touching? Think of things that make you feel safe and stable when you touch them. For example, one of my favorite methods of grounding myself is to sink my fingers inside a bag of rice. When the cool sensation of the rice reaches my fingers, I can feel myself calming down. You might need to experiment a bit on this front, but once you find something that can be used as a grounding object, it will help you when you feel extremely anxious or stressed in the future.

Affirmations for Root Chakra Healing

We've discussed how an unbalanced root chakra can make us feel extremely unstable and insecure. Therefore, we can use the power of affirmations in order to heal our root chakra. Some of these affirmations are

- I feel deeply connected to my body at all times.
- I am safe, secure, and stable.
- I am taken care of in every way.
- I feel nourished and well-rested.
- I am able to connect easily to nature and its numerous blessings.
- I am disciplined without being rigid.
- I am able to replenish myself by connecting to the Earth.
- I believe that I can create the life I want by having faith in myself.
- I have everything I need to feel safe and happy.
- I trust in my body's wisdom at all times.
- I release fear and welcome abundance into my life.

Tools, Techniques, and Rituals for Root Chakra Healing

To understand how we can heal our root chakra, we need to become familiar with its characteristics. The root chakra is not present in our physical body, but it can be energetically located in our body for the purposes of visualization and meditation. In our physical body, we can imagine the root chakra to be located at the base of our spine. Our root chakra is related to the Earth element, which is why the above grounding techniques work best for healing it. Usually, this chakra is associated with the color red. When it comes to stones or crystals, the preferred colors are red or black.

Root Chakra Visualization

In order to heal the root chakra, you need to close your eyes and take a deep breath as you visualize the chakra in your body. Imagine it as a red spinning wheel or an intense red light that helps you connect to the Earth and get rid of all the negative energy within it. As you breathe deeply through this process, imagine that any feelings of inertia or lethargy are being replaced by strength, vitality, and purpose. Once you get comfortable imagining the root chakra in your body, you can even combine the visualization practice with the chanting of your favorite affirmations.

Yoga Poses for Root Chakra Healing

Yoga is a powerful way of connecting ourselves to our mind, body, and spirit all at once. It can be challenging for beginners or for those who aren't immersed in yogic traditions. At the same time, it's an extremely useful practice to follow for anyone who wants to advance on their spiritual journey, as long as certain things are kept in mind. In general, it's always a good idea to start your yoga practice under the supervision of an expert. If you have any pre-existing conditions—especially those that you're on medication for—always consult with your doctor before committing to this practice. Many yoga poses are helpful when it comes to issues like joint pain, but it's vital to ensure that you don't end up hurting yourself when you're just starting out. Similarly, if you've just undergone surgery, ask your doctor when it's okay for you to start practicing yoga.

If you're pregnant, certain yoga poses can be very beneficial for you, but these should never be done on your own. Yoga asanas (poses) for pregnancy are determined based on the trimester you're in, as well as the specific conditions surrounding your surgery. A doctor and an expert in yoga can together determine if you should be doing yoga at this time and then come up with a practice that suits you. If you're menstruating, it is usually safer to stop practicing for the first two to three days. If you don't have any cramps and are able to continue your practice at this time, take it easy and do not practice any inversions.

Last but not least, yoga is an intuitive practice that is meant to work with your body and not against it. Some people have greater flexibility than others when they start, and some take longer to get used to a regular yoga practice. That is perfectly okay. As long as you're tuning in to your body and showing up regularly for yourself, you don't need to rush through your practice or reach a certain level in a short amount of time. This is a lifelong practice, so every step matters.

For root chakra healing, we need to focus on poses that help us gain strength, maintain balance, and develop overall stability. Some of the best yoga poses for root chakra healing are balasana (child's pose), uttanasana (standing forward bend), virabhadrasana (warrior pose), vrksasana (tree pose), and tadasana (mountain pose).

YOGA POSES FOR ROOT CHAKRA HEALING

Yoga Poses for Root Chakra Healing

Some of the best yoga poses for root chakra healing are balasana (child's pose), uttanasana (standing forward bend), virabhadrasana (warrior pose), vrksasana (tree pose), and tadasana (mountain pose).

Healing Through Crystals

If you want to work with crystals to heal your root chakra, some of the most effective ones are red garnet, zircon, red zincite, red jasper, spinel, zircon, hematite, smoky quartz, black tourmaline, and black obsidian. When working with your body, you can place any of these stones on your feet and then meditate using your favorite techniques. You can also wear jewelry made of these stones around your ankle. Another way in which you can benefit from the healing power of crystals is by creating an altar in your home. This altar can be made by using certain crystals, as well as some elements that help ground you. You can use plants, a piece of the Earth, or even your preferred grounding objects to create this altar. This altar can serve as a safe space for you to practice your root chakra meditations, visualizations, and yoga asanas.

One of the most powerful stones that can help heal your root chakra is black obsidian. It helps protect you against gaslighting, bullying, sadness, and anything that causes illusions in your life. The snowflake obsidian, on the other hand, helps protect you against your own destructive patterns and self-limiting beliefs. Since crystals hold a lot of power, it's always advisable to work with them under the guidance of a trusted healer or spiritual advisor, especially as a beginner.

Healing Through Essential Oils

Essential oils are great if you want to center yourself and relieve stress from your body and mind. Always remember that essential oils are extremely concentrated, so never use them without carrier oils. Also, always conduct a patch test on a small area of your skin to confirm that you're not allergic to the oil. You can use essential oils in various ways on your healing journey. For example, you can apply it gently to your pressure points to help you feel calmer. You can also use a humidifier to gently disperse essential oils in your environment. You can use them while engaging in a self-care ritual—like a relaxing bath—or while taking part in meditation.

Some of the most effective essential oils for root chakra healing are lavender, sandalwood, cedarwood, clove, geranium, black pepper, frankincense, and patchouli.

Journal Prompts to Help You on Your Root Chakra Healing Journey

Before we end this chapter, let's discuss certain prompts that can help us on this journey:

- How does my body feel currently?
- How do my surroundings feel, and what can be done to make myself feel better in my surroundings?
- What are some of the limiting beliefs that are holding me back right now?
- What are some things I have always believed but no longer know to be true?
- What are three or five "true" or "real" things in my life right now?
- What are three thoughts of the past and three of the future that plague me constantly?
- What about these aspects (of the past and future) can I change, and what can I accept?
- Can I reframe my past experiences as learnings for the present and future?
- Can I take some steps today to reduce anxiety about my future? What is the smallest, most meaningful thing I can do to achieve this today?
- What is in my control at this very moment?
- What can I let go of to make myself feel less stuck right now?
- What can I do to feel more connected to myself right now?

Once we've healed our root chakra, we move on to sacral chakra healing to reclaim our creativity and emotional balance after narcissistic abuse.

Chapter 2:

Sacral Chakra Renewal— Reclaiming Emotional Balance and Creativity After Narcissistic Abuse

The creative adult is the child who survived. –Ursula K. Le Guin

In many ways, the above quote helps us understand why it's important to heal our sacral chakra, especially as we recover from a period of narcissistic abuse. The sacral chakra—also known as the swadhishtana—is the second chakra in the subtle body. This chakra is known as the seat of emotions, creativity, and sexuality. When this chakra is aligned, we are in touch with all our emotions. We're able to accept all the emotions that arise within us, and we don't feel burdened by the particularly difficult ones. At the same time, we're able to stay in touch with our sensuality and sexuality without any shame or guilt. We're willing to explore what pleasure means to us and how we can center our pleasure and needs in intimate relationships.

When our sacral chakra is out of balance, it leads to physical problems such as issues in the urinary tract and reproductive system. The areas of our body that are affected most are the lower back, hip, and pelvic region. Emotionally and spiritually, this is the chakra that channels the divine feminine energy. In other words, when this chakra is in balance, we're in a place to receive emotional and sensual energy without any fear. We're also in a state of flow, meaning we engage so deeply with ourselves and our creativity that we don't feel conscious of or constricted by matters of time and space. What happens when our sacral chakra is out of balance?

For some, this means being unable to get in touch with their emotional, creative, and sensual side. Think about how comfortable you feel talking or thinking about pleasure. How confident are you in expressing your emotions? Have you spent some time on creative projects lately? What do you do to focus on self-expression? Usually, victims of narcissistic abuse have trouble advocating for their needs in all aspects of their lives—including in emotional and sexual matters. Chances are, when you tried to tell your partner about your needs and concerns, you were not only shot down but were also made to feel guilty for having expectations. In fact, one of the strongest indications of a blocked sacral chakra is shame.

Others deal with sacral chakra imbalances by becoming too obsessed with sex. They might also be unable to control the intensity of their emotions in some cases. Healing the sacral chakra can be extremely challenging for people who have suffered narcissistic abuse because they have to contend with the prevailing narratives in their culture as well as inside their own heads. Here are a few questions that can help you identify if your sacral chakra is out of balance:

- Have my views regarding sex and pleasure changed for the negative over time?
- Do I feel ashamed when thinking or talking about pleasure?
- Do I believe that I don't deserve to "ask" for things when it comes to pleasure or emotions?
- Do I feel like I'm being clingy or desperate when I advocate for my emotional needs?
- Am I uncomfortable when expressing emotions, or do I tend to dismiss my emotions, thinking they are unwarranted?
- Am I able to express myself creatively in any way?
- Do I think of creative pursuits as a waste of time and resources?
- Do I believe that I'm simply "not good enough" to pursue creative hobbies or interests?
- Do I have an unhealthy obsession with sex?
- Am I able to get in touch with my emotions without drowning in them?

- Do I feel confident in maintaining healthy relationships with others and maintaining my sense of self in these relationships?
- Do I live in constant fear of being betrayed or hurt by those closest to me?

If more than half the answers to these questions are "yes," your sacral chakra might be seriously out of balance.

Reviving Creativity and Reconnecting With Joy

Sonia has been an overachiever all her life. Ever since she was a child, she excelled at everything she participated in—from academics to sports and from debates to art competitions. Everyone—from her parents to teachers—admired her for being an all-rounder, and she could, theoretically, have followed any path she liked. However, there was an unsaid agreement among people that she would choose the "practical" and materially rewarding field of tech as her career path. Everything else could—at best—be a hobby or an extra-curricular activity. At the time, it made sense. If she could excel at almost anything, why not excel at something that made life easier for her?

She liked many aspects of her career, learned a lot, and became financially secure. She had a lot to be thankful for in her career. Still, she couldn't help but wonder that something was missing in her life. She vaguely remembered how much joy art brought into her life, and she wanted to get in touch with that childlike wonder again. The problem was that she neither had the time nor the energy to pursue these interests after an intense day at work.

When she got together with Max, he seemed impressed by her achievements in the beginning but later used every opportunity he had to undermine her. Whenever she tried to get back to art, he would scoff at her—either by dismissing her skills or by calling her "irresponsible" or "frivolous." Slowly, Sonia distanced herself from anything that brought joy into her life, and she even bought into the idea that she had never been creative—that her entire childhood had been a fluke.

When she finally split with Max, she was eager to start her life afresh. This, however, was easier said than done. She realized that she had been out of touch with her creative self for so long that it felt like that person was as alien to her. She also realized that she had spent most of her life "proving" to others that she was good at various things. She almost felt she had to "earn" their approval to engage in activities that she liked. After her relationship with her narcissistic ex, these tendencies had increased. In the process, everything she enjoyed needed to be justified for her to enjoy it. It also put a lot of pressure on her to create something amazing instead of just thinking about how it made her feel.

It took her a long time to come to a place where she could connect creative expression to joy, authenticity, and freedom, and it happened when her daughter started showing an interest in art. As she watched her daughter take to art with glee and abandon, it reminded her of her own self. On some days, she almost envied her daughter's confidence and vowed to protect it for as long as she could. She also realized that if she could somehow focus on the joy she derived from art—rather than on thoughts around her skills—she might be able to get in touch with her own inner child.

Sacral Chakra Healing

In this section, we'll learn how to heal different aspects of our sacral chakra through various techniques.

Reconnecting With Your Emotions

Our relationship with a narcissist can affect our emotional health in various ways. We have to deal with negative self-talk and intrusive thoughts, manage our triggers, and learn to validate our emotions. Let's go through these one by one.

Challenging Negative Thoughts

There are many different kinds of negative thoughts that you might have to overcome once you've left your toxic relationship behind. When you were in a relationship with a narcissist, you might have internalized a lot of negative self-talk and limiting beliefs. Here are a few examples of such thoughts:

- I am doomed to be sad, angry, or anxious for the rest of my life.
- I am responsible for everything bad that is happening or has happened to me.
- I am ashamed of my emotions and my desires.
- I don't deserve to feel good about myself.
- Every negative thing I've heard about myself from others is true.
- I am incapable of forming and maintaining healthy relationships with others.
- I should not try to be vulnerable with others, as I'll inevitably end up getting hurt and betrayed.
- I am stupid or emotionally weak, which is why people end up taking advantage of me.

One of the most effective ways of challenging negative thoughts is to start writing these thoughts in an "emotions" journal. As you write down one of these statements, think about where these thoughts come from. When was the first time you thought this way? Who said these things to you? Here is a small exercise you can do when you feel overwhelmed with negative thoughts.

Step 1: Take a deep breath and ground yourself.

Step 2: Ask yourself where this belief originates from.

Step 3: Think for a while about examples that counter these thoughts. For example, if your internal self-talk goes I am incapable of forming and maintaining healthy relationships with others, think about one healthy and loving relationship in your life to tell yourself that these thoughts don't reflect your current truth or reality.

Step 4: As you breathe consciously, repeat gently to yourself, My thoughts are not my reality.

The Ho'oponopono Prayer for the Offended Self

When we've been hurt by our narcissistic partner in various ways, we often carry the pain and anger within us for a long time. Not only that, but we often don't get any acknowledgment or closure from the narcissist, which makes it very difficult for us to heal. In the absence of validation, we often carry a lot of blame and guilt within ourselves. We hold ourselves responsible for everything we've gone through. When we are unable to forgive ourselves—and others—we have difficulty experiencing peace and love in our lives.

Before we talk about the beautiful Hawaiian prayer known as Ho'oponopono, let's first discuss why forgiveness is such a powerful concept for those who want to heal from trauma and abuse. Forgiveness isn't a sign of weakness on our part. Those who forgive don't have to forget what happened to them, but they no longer want to be controlled by that incident or person. In other words, they take back the power that a particular person or event has on them.

Also, when we're struggling to forgive others for their behavior toward us, we might also be struggling to give ourselves grace. We might not be able to give ourselves the love and kindness we deserve, especially after it was denied to us by those we trusted and looked up to. This prayer sets us free from the cycle of guilt and self-blame and makes it possible for us to love ourselves and others again. Ho'oponopono translates roughly to "restoring balance in our lives and relationships." It contains the elements of forgiveness, gratitude, and love within itself.

Here's how you can perform this simple ritual to heal your sacral chakra:

Step 1: Sit down in a comfortable position and close your eyes.

Step 2: Take a deep breath and set an intention for this session. You can say something simple like I want to let go of the negative emotions that overwhelm me, or you can be more specific and think about the person you want to forgive. Sometimes, you might find that you need to forgive yourself more than anyone else.

Step 3: As you exhale, say this prayer out loud—"I'm sorry, please forgive me, thank you, I love you."

Step 4: Repeat this phrase at least 10 times in one session, and don't rush through it. It seems like a simple prayer, but it can take a while for its essence to reach you.

Identifying and Reintegrating Your Shadow Self

When we undergo trauma, abuse, or any kind of experience that makes us feel unsafe in any way—we hide those aspects of ourselves in our shadow self. This concept was first popularized by Carl Jung—a Swedish psychoanalyst—who tried to understand the ways in which we present ourselves to the world. He came with the concepts of "collective unconscious," "persona," "archetypes," and "shadow self." Our persona is the part of our conscious self that we present to the world. It helps us navigate this world with ease because we can adjust our persona to suit the needs of those around us. Everything that we cannot find a place for gets relegated to the shadow self. This includes feelings and behaviors that aren't considered appropriate by our elders when we're children, experiences that we would rather not remember or deal with, and desires that we've been told are wrong or misplaced.

Think of it as a mask that you use to protect yourself. For example, someone who has been in a relationship with a narcissistic ex for a while might be able to predict what sets their partner off. In order to protect themselves (and their kids), they might need to repress certain aspects of themselves. If they know that their partner will make them feel bad for expressing certain emotions or desires, they do their best to repress them. These then become a part of their shadow self. The longer their emotions are repressed, the stronger their shadow self becomes. Even if they escape the relationship, their shadow self remains intact.

How does this shadow self affect us in our daily lives? One thing to understand about the shadow self is that it doesn't necessarily contain aspects of ourselves that are negative. Instead, it contains aspects that we should embrace but cannot—thus leading to guilt, shame, and anger. For instance, if you were told by your partner that you weren't creative, you might have rejected any creative impulses within yourself. These become a part of your shadow self and have a tremendous impact on your life. For instance, you might feel triggered when you see someone boldly expressing themselves and wonder why you're feeling triggered. When we reject parts of ourselves, we don't know who we truly are. We battle guilt, anger, shame, and even depression in some cases. This affects our relationships with others and makes it difficult for us to deal with various kinds of triggers in our lives.

As you recover from narcissistic abuse, you might find yourself getting triggered more often than usual. You might find it difficult to control your emotions around people or have difficulty understanding your own. During this phase, it can be extremely helpful to work on reintegrating your shadow self into your persona. Here are a couple of exercises you can do to heal your shadow self and your sacral chakra.

Journaling About Your Emotions

A simple journaling exercise can help you identify your shadow aspects by allowing you to focus on your emotions and triggers without any judgment or guilt. The first thing you can do is "label" the emotions that surface during your interactions with others or even when you're by yourself. It's important to know exactly what you're feeling so that you can uncover the reasons behind these emotions.

Make a list of your common triggers. Don't attach any judgment to them, but be detailed about the scenarios in which these triggers occur. For instance, if you get triggered when someone repeatedly offers help (not in an annoying manner), ask yourself why you feel this way. Also, make a note of the other emotions or thoughts that accompany you during this time. Do you feel angry that someone is offering unsolicited help? If yes, why? Is it because it makes you feel vulnerable? Similarly, do you feel scared when asking someone for help? Is it because you feel like you might lose your independence in the process? You can only understand what you're truly feeling if you sit with the discomfort that surfaces at the beginning of the process.

Our shadow self forms when we reject our emotions. Therefore, being able to identify and reconcile with our emotions makes it easy for us to recognize our shadow self and also forms the basis for the reintegration of our shadow self.

Facing Your Shadow Self

An important aspect of reintegrating our shadow is being able to face it and work through the unresolved emotions and trauma that might get triggered in the process. Sometimes, it can help us to treat our shadow self as a separate entity and talk to it as if we're trying to understand its fears, motivations, and dreams. We can do this through the "empty chair exercise." In this exercise, we can imagine that our shadow self sits in an empty chair facing us. Then, we prepare a script—on our own or with the help of a therapist—which contains questions we might want to ask our shadow self or affirmations that we might like to share with them. This can take a few sessions, but over time, it can get easier for us to face the shadow aspects of ourselves.

This technique can work in another way. Often, victims of abuse (including narcissistic abuse) don't receive any closure from their abusers. This can delay healing, and it can also lead to repressed emotions that affect our mental health, relationships, and quality of life. For some of us, this can manifest as unresolved anger that is directed at those who have not hurt us. For others, it can lead to difficulties expressing ourselves in relationships and embracing our creativity. The empty chair method can help us overcome these issues by giving us an opportunity to express our emotions toward our abusers. Since we might not be able to address our actual abusers—or get the reactions we want from them—we can imagine that they occupy the chair in front of us. Then, we can work through our emotions of pain, hurt, and betrayal as we communicate with them. At the end of these sessions, we let go of the emotions that hold us back and reclaim our lives from those who have hurt us.

One thing to keep in mind is that these sessions can often be extremely intense and even upsetting to us. If you don't feel confident about navigating these difficult emotions on your own, consult your therapist and ask them to conduct these sessions with you. In general—it's advisable to engage in shadow work under the guidance of someone you trust—especially if you're a beginner.

Reconnecting With Your Creative Energy

One of the biggest blocks we face in embracing our creativity is self-doubt. We believe that only some people can be creative or that we need to have certain talents to call ourselves creative. This is absolutely not true. In fact, our creativity is unlocked when we are not self-conscious and engage in activities that bring us unconditional joy. It takes a while to remember that labels like "good" and "successful" are worldly terms that are subjective at best and inaccurate at worst. As long as we rely on external measures of creativity, we're not going to be able to experience the freedom that comes with authentic self-expression.

If you want to reconnect with your creative spirit, take a leaf out of a child's playbook. Think about an activity that you enjoyed doing as a child but grew out of as an adult. It could be anything—from drawing to writing, from building to dancing—that makes you happy. Set aside some time to engage in this activity every day (or as regularly as you can). Even if you can only give half an hour to this activity, don't worry about it. What's important is that you focus exclusively on it during the time you've set aside for it. For the first few days or weeks, I'd suggest that you do this activity alone—just so that you gain some confidence in yourself and free yourself from judgment. Once you've gotten used to this activity, you can invite someone you love and trust to do this activity with you. What's more, you can also switch between activities as and when you please. The important thing is to explore as much as you can and to know yourself in the process. In fact, "art therapy" is already considered by many healers and therapists as a way for people to express their deepest emotions and to heal their shadow selves. Find out what gives voice to your repressed emotions and desires, and engage with them as much as you can.

Reconnecting With Your Sensuality Through Self-Care

In the last chapter, we used our senses to ground ourselves in the present moment. In this chapter, our senses help us reconnect with our sensuality. When our body is used to being in constant fight-flight-fawn-or-freeze mode, we often have difficulty connecting with our sensual selves. As we recover from abuse, it might be challenging for us to go through even the most basic self-care routines. However, if we establish certain self-care rituals and make them a part of our daily lives, our body finds it easier to get into rest-and-relaxation mode. Getting in touch with our sensuality also helps us get rid of shame and find our capacity for joy and pleasure in the smallest things.

Let's go through a simple sensual self-care ritual:

- Prepare a warm bath using essential oils and fragrances, and use it to relax either in the morning or after a long day.
- Spend as much as you can in nature—through hiking, forest bathing, or activities like birdwatching. Let your senses immerse themselves in the beauty of the natural world.
- Choose an activity that pleasantly engages your senses. For example, you can spend some time cooking your favorite meals, preferably something that takes time to cook. This way, you can enjoy the colors, textures, and flavors of the meal even before you've eaten it.

Affirmations for Sacral Chakra Healing

Here are some affirmations that can help us heal our sacral chakra and reconnect us with our emotions, sensuality, and creativity:

- My emotions are real and valid, and I embrace all of them.

- I release those emotions that don't serve me anymore.
- I embrace all the changes in my life and acknowledge the growth that comes with these changes.
- My emotions teach me about myself and I am grateful for each one of them.
- I am a creative being, and my creative energy flows freely through me.
- I am capable of recognizing and fulfilling all my passions.
- I am in touch with my sensuality and with everything that brings me joy.
- I let go of all shame, guilt, and anger toward myself and others.
- I deserve love, pleasure, and emotional well-being.
- I accept all parts of myself—even the difficult and repressed parts.

Tools, Techniques, and Rituals for Sacral Chakra Healing

In our energetic body, the sacral chakra is located just below the navel and has an effect on our lower back, reproductive system, and urinary tract. It's represented by the water element, which is why we can use the healing effect of water to bring our sacral chakra back into balance. The color most associated with this chakra is orange. We can use this knowledge to create our very own healing rituals for the sacral chakra.

Sacral Chakra Visualization

Sit in a comfortable position with your spine upright. Make sure that your spine is relaxed. Close your eyes and visualize a spinning wheel or a light of bright orange color just below your navel. As you breathe out, get rid of any emotions like guilt or anger that might be holding you back. If you feel any guilt around your desires or emotions, peacefully let them go and replace them with feelings of joy, pleasure, creative energy, and acceptance as you inhale.

Another technique that can help you balance your sacral chakra is incorporating water into your visualizations. You can either do your meditation and visualization practice near a body of water—simply having a bowl of water near you when you meditate also works—or you can do a visualization exercise where you find yourself on the beach or beside a stream. It can also help to listen to the sounds of the waves or the stream in the background. As you allow the healing energy of water to flow through your senses, you can reconnect with all aspects of your divine feminine energy.

Yoga Poses for Sacral Chakra Healing

When it comes to sacral chakra healing, we need to focus on poses that are more hip-focused—as they can help unblock our emotions as well as our sensual and creative energy. We want our hips to be open and strong without being too tight or too loose. Some of the best yoga poses for sacral chakra healing are utkata Konasana (Goddess pose), virasana (Hero's pose), mandukasana (frog pose), paschimottanasana (seated forward fold), and prasarita padottanasana (wide-legged forward fold).

YOGA POSES FOR SACRAL CHAKRA HEALING

Yoga Poses for Sacral Chakra Healing

Some of the best yoga poses for sacral chakra healing are utkata Konasana (Goddess pose), virasana (Hero's pose), mandukasana (frog pose), paschimottanasana (seated forward fold), and prasarita padottanasana (wide-legged forward fold).

Healing Through Crystals

One of the most powerful crystals for sacral chakra healing is the moonstone. This crystal is connected to the divine feminine energy, which is also related to the healing energy of the moon. Another crystal that helps enhance our emotional and sensual well-being is the orange calcite. While the rhodonite helps release negative emotions and practice forgiveness, the carnelian helps enhance both emotional stability and creativity. Some other crystals that can be used in this process are amber, sunstone, fire opal, orange selenite, orange sapphire, and orange tourmaline.

Healing Through Essential Oils

Some of the most effective essential oils for healing the sacral chakra are patchouli, sweet orange, tangerine, rose, ylang-ylang, and pink pepper seed.

Journal Prompts to Help You on Your Sacral Chakra Healing Journey

Here are a few journal prompts that can help you on your sacral chakra journey:

- What are the emotions I am currently experiencing?
- Which of my emotions am I struggling to embrace and why?
- What are three things that I feel most guilty about?
- What are my limiting beliefs around creativity?
- What are my thoughts on pleasure and sensuality, and what are some aspects of my sensuality that I struggle with?
- What are some behaviors that trigger me and why?
- Are there any memories that I have repressed or any emotions that I deny within myself?
- How can I channel my creativity in a healthy manner?

- What are some emotions I need to let go and what is holding me back from doing so?
- Is there someone I need to forgive in order to heal myself?
- What are some ways in which I can practice sensual self-care in my life?
- Now that we've healed our sacral chakra, let's move on to the solar plexus chakra—the seat of our personal power.

Chapter 3:

Solar Plexus Chakra Healing—Rebuilding Your Confidence and Self-Esteem After Narcissistic Abuse

You have power over your mind—not outside events. Realize this, and you will find strength. –Marcus Aurelius

The third chakra in our subtle body—also known as the manipura—is the seat of personal power. Located above the navel, this chakra governs our confidence, resilience, self-esteem, and sense of purpose. It's connected to the fire element, which is where it gets its energy from. Physically, this chakra is responsible for our digestive health. Emotionally and mentally, it is responsible for our "sense of self."

When this chakra is in balance, we feel confident in our intellect. We also become clear about our purpose and gain the willpower and discipline needed to fulfill that purpose. In our relationships—both personal and professional—we are able to assert ourselves without getting aggressive. When this chakra is out of alignment, however, it can lead to a host of physical, mental, and emotional problems.

To understand this, we need to understand that this chakra is connected to our ego. In spiritual parlance, this word is often used condescendingly because, after all, we need to dissolve our ego to attain ultimate spiritual union. However, our ego isn't the villain it's often made out to be. No matter what our path is, we need to maintain a balance between our material and spiritual goals. Our ego helps us navigate the material or physical world with relative ease. It provides us with the sense of self—the "I"—needed to understand where we belong in this world.

Having a healthy sense of ego means that we know our place in this world and are not afraid of claiming it. We have high self-worth and self-esteem, and we have the optimism and resilience needed to face challenges that inevitably come our way. When we have to deal with a narcissistic partner, our self-worth takes a massive hit. Think about it this way. On one hand, a narcissist has an inflated sense of ego—which makes them think and act as if they're the center of the world. On the other hand, they need the world around them—including their partner—to reinforce their erroneous beliefs about themselves. In order to achieve this, they need to undermine their partner's self-worth and blame them for anything that goes wrong in their relationship. Add to that the constant gaslighting—as well as the fawn response that many victims use to appease their partner and defuse potentially dangerous situations—and it's no wonder that it takes years for many of us to reclaim our sense of self even after leaving a toxic relationship.

An out-of-balance solar plexus chakra can lead to physical problems such as indigestion, irritable bowel syndrome, ulcers, excessive weight gain, eating disorders, diabetes, sensitive gums, heartburn, and problems in the colon, liver, and pancreas. Many of these gut-related issues can also lead to mental health issues like anxiety and depression, as well as skin problems. Emotionally, an imbalance in this chakra leads to feelings of insecurity, low self-worth, and purposelessness. We might have trouble setting boundaries in our lives, and we might indulge in people-pleasing behaviors in order to get approval from them. In some cases, we might become too aggressive with others, and we might also have issues with control. A blocked solar plexus chakra also implies that we might have trouble making decisions in our lives.

Here are a few questions that can help you identify whether your solar plexus chakra is out of balance:

- Am I able to assert myself in my relationships—both personal and professional?
- Am I triggered more easily than usual into lashing out at others?
- Do I keep quiet when I need to speak up, or am I allowing people to treat me poorly?
- Do I believe that I deserve poor treatment from others?

- Do I frequently give in to others' views just to ensure that they aren't upset with me?
- Do I frequently feel directionless, hopeless, or helpless in life?
- Am I overly sensitive to criticism—even if I know it's coming from a place of genuine concern?
- Do I have trouble trusting myself or others?
- Do I feel like I don't have control over my own life?
- Am I rigid in my decisions, or do I try to exercise control over other people's lives?
- Do I have a poor opinion of my skills and attributes?
- Do I struggle to believe that I can face the challenges life throws at me?

If the answers to more than half of these questions are "yes," then your solar plexus chakra might be out of balance.

Building Resilience and Reclaiming Confidence

Patricia would like to believe that she was a confident child and teenager, though she has trouble remembering who she was before the relationship that nearly destroyed her sense of self. Years of trying to appease her ex—who, of course, wouldn't be happy no matter what—made her doubt whether she was good enough for anything. The most significant effect she felt was on her ability to make decisions—both in her personal and professional life. She found herself stuck in a pattern of analysis paralysis every time she had to make a choice. If she did make a decision on time, she would second-guess herself so much that it was exhausting. Every so often, she felt so scared about making choices that they didn't feel like decisions anymore. It was like the voice of her ex was always around—admonishing her and telling her all the ways in which she was unworthy. These feelings didn't subside when she managed to do something well and was lauded for it. In fact, she felt more like an imposter when this happened and spent her day anxious that she might be "found out."

When Patricia realized that—even though her relationship was over—she hadn't truly escaped its shadow—it became clear to her that she hadn't healed from the trauma that her ex had inflicted on her. She knew she had to build her self-worth from the ground up, but she kept hitting a wall. As she put herself through therapy, she came to an epiphany about herself. All her life, she had believed that confidence and resilience were qualities you were either born with or you weren't. It didn't help that her ex frequently commented on how she lacked confidence after undermining her, thus making his erosion of her self-esteem her fault.

Her therapist pointed out to her that resilience is a muscle—something that can become stronger and more effective the more it is used. Seen through this lens, Patricia gained a new perspective on her problems. While she didn't welcome them, she was able to see them as opportunities to train her "resilience muscle." Over time, she began to see problems not as events that happened to her—or even because of her—but for her. This didn't mean that she needed to be grateful for the challenges in her life. At the same time, she could stop seeing them as a burden anymore. Patricia realized that the fog of trauma that hung over her life till then had kept her from gaining much-needed perspective on herself and her problems—and she was finally determined to change that.

Solar Plexus Chakra Healing

In this section, we'll discuss various techniques that can help us heal our solar plexus chakra and reclaim our personal power.

Understanding and Building Resilience

In the case study, we talked about the "resilience muscle" that we all possess but need to exercise at times. What does it mean to be resilient? Think of it this way. Two siblings who have grown up in the same environment at home—and a similar one at school—can have very different reactions to a difficult situation. For instance, if they're struggling with a subject at school, one might think about ways to bridge this gap by asking for help from others. The other sibling might either give up entirely or they might buckle under the stress. What is behind this difference in reactions?

A resilient person is able to come back from a difficult situation, while a non-resilient person struggles to do so. In fact, resilient people see setbacks and challenges as opportunities to learn and grow. This does not mean that they're unreasonably positive all the time or that they don't feel stressed, angry, or anxious during these times. It simply means that they honor these emotions without letting them dictate their lives. There are many factors that contribute to a person's resilience. While genetics and environment play a significant role, resilience isn't a fixed quality. Sure, some people might be born more resilient than others, but anyone can train themselves to become more resilient over time.

When we've gone through years of abuse—and have probably been told that we deserve it—we often lose hope and start believing that we're always going to feel scared, miserable, or helpless. Building resilience helps decenter the abuse (and the abuser) from our lives—thus gaining control of our narrative and focusing on our healing and growth.

Here are a few aspects of resilience that we might need to work on:

- **Our sense of control:** When faced with a problem, do we believe that we have control over the situation? If we have faith that we can handle a difficult situation ourselves, we have an "internal locus of control." If, on the other hand, we think that our circumstances will get the better of us—we have an "external locus of control." For people healing from narcissistic abuse—it can be difficult to keep the focus exclusively on ourselves—especially when we do have someone else to blame for a lot of our troubles. Having an internal locus of control doesn't mean that we ignore our circumstances or the people who have hurt us. It simply means that we don't feel powerless in the face of this knowledge.

- **Mental and emotional clarity:** When faced with challenges, our emotions overwhelm us to the point that they distort our thoughts and behaviors. These cognitive and emotional distortions make us indulge in catastrophizing (believing that things are worse than they are), all-or-nothing thinking (thinking in extremes), or overgeneralization (taking one instance and imagining a pattern around it). Resilient people can acknowledge their challenges and weaknesses without giving in to cognitive distortions. For example, if something goes wrong at work, they can make a list of things that could have been done better rather than saying something like *I always make mistakes; I'm simply not good at this job.*

- **Emotional regulation:** When we achieve mental and emotional clarity, we're able to regulate our emotions in a healthy manner. Not only that, but we can also assess other people's emotions and make decisions that prioritize our well-being without compromising on theirs. For instance, if someone criticizes us, we can respond to their criticism without taking it personally and without getting aggressive in return.

- **Interdependence in relationships:** Resilient people are able to maintain their independence while also building a community around them. They understand that strength and vulnerability are not opposites of each other. In fact, one makes the other possible. Therefore, they can ask for help from others when needed, and they truly believe that they're worthy of support at all times.

- **Problem-solving skills:** Resilient people focus on how to solve their problems instead of getting intimidated by them. This also means that they have the ability to look at their problems through a different lens. They can reframe challenges as opportunities and difficult experiences as lessons.

- **Confidence in our ability to overcome challenges:** Our mindset determines how we deal with problems in our lives. If we possess a "victim mentality," we're going to stay in the energy of blaming others for the challenges in our lives. We might have difficulty healing from the trauma inflicted on us, and we might see everything through the lens of pain, anger, and fear. This does not mean that healing happens overnight or that we need to rush the process of recovery. What it means is that we acknowledge the setbacks and obstacles encountered during this process without seeing them as signs of failure or weakness. In other words, what we need is a "warrior mindset."

- **Fierce self-compassion:** Self-compassion is all about giving ourselves the grace and love that we haven't received from our ex and maybe even from others. Self-compassion helps us be gentle with ourselves when things get tough, while fierce self-compassion combines the "warrior mindset" with love, patience, and kindness toward ourselves. Fierce self-compassion—a concept popularized by Kristen Neff in her book of the same name—allows us to be honest about our trauma and suffering, hold others accountable for how they've treated us, and take action to protect ourselves from further harm. For some, fierce self-compassion is what allows them to offer help and support to others who might be dealing with similar trauma and suffering.

- **Having a "growth" mindset:** Psychologist and author Carol Dweck came up with the twin concepts of "growth" and "fixed" mindsets. While people with fixed mindsets believe that they have a fixed set of skills, talents, or even opportunities to make their mark on this world, those with growth mindsets understand that they have the ability to influence their own destinies. They see challenges as learning opportunities, and they also understand that their own identity isn't set in stone. Therefore, those with a growth mindset are naturally resilient because they don't see problems or bad experiences as the end of the world.

Ways to Build Resilience

Here are a few ways in which we can build resilience within ourselves.

Practicing Fierce Self-Compassion

Fierce self-compassion is something that we might need to learn, especially as we recover from narcissistic abuse. This is because, in the aftermath of the trauma—we might struggle to stand up for ourselves, draw boundaries in our relationships, and look beyond the pain we're experiencing in the moment. We might also center the abuse and the abuser too much—so much so that it threatens our emotional stability. This is a simple exercise that anyone can do when they feel triggered or threatened, and it takes about 5–10 minutes. Also, since resilience is a muscle that you need to keep working on—it's a good idea to practice as regularly as possible, even when you're not especially triggered. This is because when you don't actually perceive a great danger to yourself— you can spend time learning the basics of this method, and you can also afford to make mistakes. Then, when you really need it, you can use these skills to ground yourself when you feel attacked or overwhelmed (*Fierce Self-Compassion Break, 2023*).

Step 1: Take a deep breath and think about the problem you're currently facing. This problem could be related to someone treating you poorly, dismissing your opinions, or disrespecting your boundaries.

Step 2: As you think about the problem, you're likely going to feel a lot of emotions. Allow yourself to feel these emotions, but don't dwell on them for long. Grounding techniques can help you achieve this balance. And this is important: While you might be tempted to focus on the *person* who is making life difficult for you, it's not useful to do so when you're trying to heal. Therefore, as much as possible, keep the focus on your own feelings instead of the person behind this.

Step 3: Once you've acknowledged your emotions, you need to validate them. In other words, you need to assure yourself that what you're feeling is real. This is especially important if you're used to having your thoughts and emotions undermined by others. For example, you can say to yourself—*I have every reason to feel threatened by this person's lack of boundaries, or I deserve to be treated with respect and consideration under all circumstances.*

Step 4: When we feel threatened or targeted by someone, it's possible to also feel lonely. When we feel lonely—or victimized as an individual—it's difficult to imagine a time when our problems will be resolved. Hence, it helps to remind ourselves that there are others in the world who are going through similar problems and are trying their best to improve their circumstances. Not only does this give us hope, but it also provides much-needed perspective.

Step 5: Once we've calmed down a little, we need to prepare ourselves to tackle these challenges head-on. You can do this by assuming a strong and confident pose—your warrior pose—in front of a mirror. You can come up with a pose that makes you feel confident, or you can simply stand with your legs hip-width apart, roll your shoulders back, and stand with your spine straight. After that, put a closed fist gently over your heart and repeat an affirmation of your choice. For instance, you can tell yourself—*I'm going to establish strong boundaries in my relationships, and those who disrespect my boundaries have no place in my life.* Once you've repeated your affirmation, put your other hand over your fist in an act of support, encouragement, and compassion.

This deceptively simple exercise balances both compassion and a warrior-like spirit to help us become more resilient over time.

Learning Problem-Solving Skills

Some of the most common problems that we might need to face as we recover from narcissistic abuse are—handling conflicts and drawing boundaries, dealing with social and familial pressure, and taking space in the world as an individual. If we have kids, it also becomes our responsibility to ensure that they are protected at all costs. If you feel overwhelmed thinking about the various problems that can arise, develop your problem-solving skills so that you can tackle them without losing your peace.

The first step is to identify the problem you're facing. Classify whether this is a new problem or a recurrent one and whether it's extremely urgent to find a solution to it or not. These classifications help us understand how much of our mental and emotional energy should be dedicated to a particular problem. For instance, if a particular person has been disrespecting your boundaries for a while—even if you've tried to explain your need for boundaries to them—you might need to take extreme measures like cutting them off or maintaining as little contact with them as possible. You might also have to implement these changes as quickly as possible to protect your emotional health.

Once you've identified the problem, figure out whether the problem is indeed solvable. For instance, if you need a job and have to work with someone for the next year or so, you cannot choose to antagonize that person unless they're disrespecting you too much. In other words, you might have to ignore certain things or make your peace with some behaviors (based on your personal boundaries). In other cases, you can and should take action as soon as possible. Knowing how to distinguish between the two can make a world of difference to your mental and emotional health.

Draw boundaries where necessary. Having boundaries in place helps you in multiple ways. These boundaries condition your mind to understand what is okay and what isn't on a daily basis. The same boundary can help in various aspects of your life. For example, if you feel triggered when someone raises their voice at you—you need to communicate the same in your personal as well as professional relationships. Similarly, if you like to have some time to yourself—you'll look for work–life balance as a professional and for "me time" in your personal relationships.

Also, boundaries help us anticipate problems in our lives. For example, if you know that your family members are still supportive of your ex, you might need to draw boundaries with them as well. You can maintain minimal contact with them—on your own terms—and you can also let them know why you're doing so. This makes it difficult for others to disrespect you in the guise of ignorance.

Once you've evaluated the alternatives available to you, implement the solution that works best for you. Be prepared for the fallout from your decision. Often, we struggle to implement boundaries even though we know how they help us. This is because those who deserve these boundaries are usually the same people who shame us for maintaining them. They might act as if you're the one disrespecting them or your relationship with them. They might make you feel ashamed for putting up these boundaries. Instead of allowing these emotions to overwhelm you, use them as signs that you need to distance yourself from such people. A powerful way of reframing boundaries is that boundaries aren't something that you do to other people but something you do for yourself. Those who see it as an act of self-care cherish you, and those who see it as an insult to themselves don't really care about your well-being in the first place.

The last aspect of problem-solving is being able to evaluate your decisions and revisit them if you need to. This can also mean asking for feedback from people you trust. Remember this: Resilience is not rigidity. One of the main reasons why resilient people can bounce back from difficult situations is that they're flexible and willing to learn from their mistakes. A truly resilient person will make confident decisions but will also be able to admit that they should take a different path when needed.

Affirmations for Solar Plexus Chakra Healing

Here are some affirmations that can help us heal our solar plexus chakra and build confidence, resilience, and self-esteem:

- I am enough.
- I am proud of my abilities and decisions.
- I trust my intuition when making choices for myself.
- I am calm, confident, and powerful, and I can handle challenges with grace and grit.
- I know my purpose in life, and I'm committed to fulfilling it at all costs.
- I am a powerful being, and I don't give my power to people or situations that don't deserve it.
- I accept all that happens to me—the good and the bad—and learn from all my experiences.

- I believe in myself and don't need the approval of others to feel good about myself.
- I have the wisdom to understand what I cannot change and the courage to change what I can.
- I cannot control how others treat me, but I can control how I react to them.
- I draw boundaries in my relationships because I respect my time and energy.
- I trust in my well of inner strength and personal power and can draw from it when faced with challenges.
- I am always worthy of love, kindness, and respect.

Tools, Techniques, and Rituals for Solar Plexus Chakra Healing

As we've discussed earlier, the solar plexus chakra is represented by the fire element. It's also depicted using the color yellow. Let's discuss a few ways in which we can balance our solar plexus chakra.

Solar Plexus Chakra Visualization

There are a few visualization exercises we can do to balance our solar plexus chakra. In the first exercise, you need to sit comfortably with your spine straight as you visualize a bright yellow light emanating from your solar plexus chakra. Allow that light to fill you with confidence, power, and resilience. As you exhale, allow all your self-doubt and anger to leave your energetic body. As you inhale, let yourself feel empowered and ready to take on life's challenges.

Another exercise can be done by utilizing the power of the sun. If you can, try to do this exercise in the morning—preferably within half an hour of sunrise. Allow the energy of the sun to emanate from your solar chakra, and chant your affirmations as you see the rays of the sun growing stronger. If you don't have proper access to sunlight where you live, you can also use a candle for this exercise.

The solar plexus chakra is connected to our "inner warrior," so we can heal this chakra by channeling this energy. For this, you can stand in front of a mirror with your spine straight and your legs shoulder-width apart. As you exhale, allow all the anger, pain, and memories of abuse to leave your body and mind. As you inhale, imagine yourself as a powerful warrior who protects you and prepares you for all the challenges that might come your way. You can also pair this exercise with one or more of the affirmations mentioned in the previous section.

Yoga Poses for Solar Plexus Chakra Healing

Since the solar plexus chakra is related to the fire element, asanas that channel the sun's energy are extremely useful in healing it. The most important among these are *surya namaskars* (sun salutations). Also, since this is a chakra related to the digestive system as well as to our inner strength—the focus should be on asanas that strengthen the core and stimulate our *jatharagni* (digestive fire). Some of the most effective poses for this chakra are *virabhadrasana* (warrior pose) I and II, *paripurna navasana* (boat pose), *bhujangasana* (cobra pose), and *dhanurasana* (bow pose).

YOGA POSES FOR SOLAR PLEXUS CHAKRA HEALING

Yoga Poses for Solar Plexus Chakra Healing

Some of the most effective poses for this chakra are virabhadrasana (warrior pose) I and II, navasana (boat pose), bhujangasana (cobra pose), and dhanurasana (bow pose).

Healing Through Crystals

Yellow crystals are the most effective in healing our solar plexus chakra. For example, the golden tiger eye is a chakra associated with the sun and solar plexus chakra. It can help enhance mental clarity, emotional balance, and personal power. Citrine is another crystal that can help release negative energy and trauma. It's also believed to help in increasing our self-esteem. Some other crystals that help improve our self-esteem and confidence are yellow calcite, golden mookaite, yellow jasper, amber, sunstone, yellow sapphire, golden topaz, yellow tourmaline, and pyrite.

Healing Through Essential Oils

Some of the most effective essential oils in solar plexus chakra healing are ginger, black pepper, cypress, geranium, mandarin, peppermint, juniper berry, sandalwood, rosemary, and Atlas cedarwood.

Journal Prompts to Help You on Your Solar Plexus Chakra Healing Journey

Before we discuss some prompts that can help you build your self-esteem and confidence, I would like to discuss a nuance that has helped me on my own solar plexus chakra healing journey. Usually, the terms self-esteem and self-worth are used interchangeably, and they are similar in most aspects. That being said, there's a small but significant difference between the two. While self-esteem has to do with our talents and contributions to the world—and can often depend on how the world perceives us—self-worth is largely an internal construct. Not only that, our self-worth doesn't depend on what we are good at or how we contribute to society. In fact, the concept of self-worth tells us that we're worthy of love and respect simply because we're human beings. This difference is extremely helpful to remember, especially when our circumstances don't allow us to be especially productive. So, if you feel like you're not especially productive at times—especially when you're focusing on your healing journey—give yourself grace and tell yourself that you're still worthy of all the good things in your life.

Here are a few prompts to help you on your solar plexus chakra healing journey:

- What past challenges have you faced in your life, and how did you overcome them?
- What are some of your greatest strengths, and how have they helped you throughout life?
- What weaknesses or limiting beliefs hold you back, and how do you plan on overcoming them?
- What goals or dreams do you have—especially those that you haven't focused on until now?
- What are some compliments or kind comments that you've received about yourself?
- What criticisms (in good faith) have you received about yourself?
- What are your deepest fears and insecurities, where do they originate from, and what can you do to overcome them?
- What mistakes have you made in the past, and how have they helped you grow and evolve over time?
- What are some ways in which you can show kindness and grace to yourself, especially during difficult times?
- If you were talking to a close friend, how would you speak to them? Do you speak to yourself in a similar manner?
- How has past trauma and abuse affected your self-esteem, and what can you do to improve it?
- What are some difficult situations that you have recovered from, and how?
- What can you do to become more resilient over time?
- What are some scenarios where you've felt disrespected, ignored, or abused?
- What boundaries do you need to draw to feel respected in your relationships?

Now that we've reclaimed our personal power through solar plexus chakra healing, let's rediscover love and compassion through the heart chakra.

Chapter 4:

Healing the Heart—Rebuilding Love and Compassion After Narcissistic Abuse

When you arise in the morning, think of what a precious privilege it is to be alive—to breathe, to think, to enjoy, to love. –Marcus Aurelius

We now move on to the fourth chakra in the subtle body—also known as anahata. The heart chakra is located in the chest region, close to the physical heart in our body. This is a very important chakra because it acts as a bridge between the "higher" and "lower" chakras. The three chakras that we've discussed until now are mostly rooted in the physical realm, while the ones after this are more concerned with spiritual growth. Don't get me wrong—every chakra has a physical and spiritual aspect to it, and we cannot access the higher chakras without our lower chakras being in balance. Therefore, our chakras don't really have any hierarchy, even though it might seem that way. Once we've aligned the three "physical" chakras, we signal our readiness for spiritual growth by aligning our heart chakra.

The word anahata means "unstruck" or "unhurt." This chakra is associated with unconditional joy, love, and compassion. When this chakra is in balance, we're able to unconditionally love ourselves and others, move away from past traumas and pain, and experience deep connections with the world around us. An aligned heart chakra allows us to access our most vulnerable selves without worrying about getting hurt or betrayed. To better understand how the heart chakra operates, we need to understand the true essence of the word "unconditional." The concept of unconditional love or joy means that we don't need to do something or be someone to be worthy of these emotions. I would even say that true love or joy is, by nature, unconditional. Everything else can feel like a transaction and a lopsided one at that.

Those of us who've been at the receiving end of narcissistic abuse probably know the word "conditional" all too well. We've likely been made to feel that we have to work hard to deserve our ex's attention, love, and concern. When our partner withheld affection from us in the past, we were made to feel like it was our fault. In fact, a relationship based on narcissistic abuse can put our heart chakra out of balance for the longest time. When this chakra is out of alignment, we live with a constant fear of rejection, which also means that we unconsciously reject ourselves.

On one hand, we might have trouble loving and trusting others and even have issues with hyper-independence. It might be difficult for us to open up and be vulnerable with others. On the other hand, we might give too much of ourselves to the point that we don't know how to receive love in a healthy manner. We might get too attached to the people in our lives and get into codependent relationships. While these two kinds of behaviors present as two extremes, they usually come from the same place: fear, grief, and insecurity. Physically, an imbalanced heart chakra can lead to heart disease, heart palpitations, lung disease, and problems in the lymphatic system, chest, upper back, and shoulders. It can also sometimes cause pain in our arms and wrists.

Here are a few questions that can help you identify whether your heart chakra is out of balance:

- Do I believe that all relationships are, ultimately, transactional?
- Do I take extreme measures to "protect" myself from people?
- Do I enter new relationships expecting to be hurt or let down?
- Do I believe that I have to look a certain way, achieve certain things, and fulfill certain expectations in order to be loved and cherished by others?
- Do I have deep trust issues that rear their heads every now and then?
- Do I blame myself when things don't work out for me in relationships?

- Do I feel like I need to do everything myself and that I cannot rely on anyone for help or support?
- Do I get too attached to people early on and have difficulty regulating my emotions around those I love?
- Do I find myself repeating the same toxic patterns that I've experienced in my previous relationships?
- Do I become distant or shut myself down when I feel threatened or misunderstood by those I love?
- Do I project a tough exterior and have my walls up most of the time?
- Do I have trouble moving on from my past relationships?
- If the answers to more than half of these questions are "Yes," then your heart chakra might be out of balance.

Reclaiming Self-Love and Healing Abandonment Wounds

If there's one word that Diana has been intimate with most of her life, it's "abandonment." What's worse is that she has experienced the kind of abandonment that doesn't come with physical absence. She grew up with two parents who fought constantly but stayed together "for her sake." She was provided for and taken care of to the best of their economic capacity, but she struggled to feel loved and cherished by them. It wasn't even that they resented her, but simply that two deeply unhappy people were unable to take care of their daughter in a healthy manner. This relationship set the tone for most of the relationships in her adult life, which is likely why she was unable to recognize the signs of narcissistic abuse in her marriage for a long time.

Try as she might, she was unable to get over the feeling that there was something wrong with her, something that made her unlovable. Also, her abandonment wounds made her extremely conscious about never making someone else feel the same way. Thus, she fell into a pattern of "over-giving" and "barely expecting anything in return." When her ex withdrew from her or withheld affection from her, she told herself that it was because she was being "too needy." When he acted affectionately toward her, she would desperately try to behave in the same manner in the future—in order to ensure that she received a constant supply of his love and care. Since she had never known a healthy model of love, she wasn't able to tell the real thing from its cheap substitute.

Even when she was able to finally leave that abusive relationship behind for good, she still struggled with healing her deep-seated abandonment wounds. Slowly, she understood that she was repeating similar patterns of behavior in her current platonic relationships as well. Maybe she always had. Because she was so particular about not hurting others, she would willingly give away all her time and energy to them. She was always the shoulder to cry on, the patient ear for everyone's problems, and the person to come to when someone felt unloved. She was always admired for these qualities, and to an outsider, she was always surrounded by friends. She had usually been called "low-maintenance" by friends and lovers alike—except in her narcissistic relationship, of course—and she wore it as a badge of honor.

It was only after leaving her abusive relationship that she was able to realize something: In her efforts not to abandon others, she had often abandoned herself. She was so careful about not inconveniencing others that she had started to exist on the periphery of her own existence. She had forgotten to take care of herself and give herself the love and kindness that she often gave to others around her. She had often felt guilty about prioritizing herself in the past, but now, she understood that she could not be truly present for anyone else unless she took care of herself first. It was going to be a long road to healing, but knowing that she deserved love and respect in all her relationships—including the one she had with herself—was a great first start.

Heart Chakra Healing

In this section, we'll discuss various techniques that can help us heal our heart chakra and reconnect with the true essence of love.

Cutting Cords and Healing Heart Wounds

The biggest barrier to heart chakra healing is grief. In this case, we can be grieving over lost relationships as well as our lost selves. Each time we leave a relationship behind, we also lose a part of ourselves. Even if this transition is necessary—and this loss is really a transformation—it can be a while before we get over this grief. Sometimes—especially in the case of abuse—there's a sense of guilt and regret over having "wasted" our time on someone who didn't deserve our love. The thing is, no matter how valid our anger or resentment might be, it ultimately holds us back from opening up our hearts to this world. How can we move on from these feelings and let go of anything that blocks our heart chakra?

Reframing Our Past Relationships

If a relationship still has its hold over you, try to look at it from a different perspective with the help of a journaling exercise.

Step 1: Think about the positive aspects of this relationship.

When were you most fulfilled during this relationship? What made you happy? Now, think about the ways in which you can find happiness on your own. How can you be more fulfilled as an individual? What are some ways in which you can connect with yourself? For example, if you enjoyed the times when your partner cared for you, why not set up a self-care routine for yourself?

Step 2: Think about the qualities that you admired in your previous partner. If you have difficulty thinking of any, think of the ideal qualities you would like in a potential partner.

Whether you found these qualities in another person or not, these are the qualities you are most attracted to. Now, ask yourself if you have the same qualities within yourself. If not, take this as an opportunity to develop them and grow as a person. When we pay attention to the vibrations we send out into the universe, we also determine the kind of energy we attract in our lives.

Step 3: Think about the worst qualities in your ex or the behaviors you had difficulty adjusting to.

These are qualities that you would not want in a future partner, nor would you like to tolerate them in your other relationships. Use your past experiences as lessons, and think about the boundaries you need to create in your life, as well as the people or energies you need to reject going forward.

This simple but profound exercise can help us use our past experiences to determine how to better love ourselves and others in the present and future. This way, they serve their purpose in your current life, thus making it easier for you to move on from them.

Practicing Metta Meditation

Metta meditation is a powerful practice that heals our heart chakra in various ways. For one, it's a method that we can use to practice self-compassion. Also, it can help us forgive those who have hurt us and who might not have provided us with the closure we needed from them. After some practice, we can use this exercise to connect with the world around us. Metta is a word from the Pali language, and it holds multiple meanings, such as benevolence, amity, goodwill, and loving-kindness. In other words, metta meditation can be seen as a way to get in touch with our ability to love unconditionally. Metta meditation is an important part of Buddhist traditions, but anyone can follow this simple practice in their lives.

Step 1: Find a comfortable position to sit, and then close your eyes.

Step 2: Take a few deep breaths and allow yourself to connect to your feelings.

Step 3: Focus on one person at a time, especially as a beginner. This is because you might get overwhelmed if you're directing your energies toward too many people at the same time.

Step 4: In the beginning, choose someone who you love or feel warmth toward. This is because it can be challenging for us to direct kind energies toward those who have hurt us when we're just starting out.

Note: Usually, the practice is to start with ourselves and then move outward—meaning, we move on to people who are closest to us, then to acquaintances, and then to strangers who might have helped us in any way. In the end, we focus our attention on people who have hurt or disappointed us. The idea is that the positive feelings generated throughout the exercise can make us feel kinder toward the people we have trouble forgiving. If you're struggling with self-compassion, you can also start with someone you love dearly.

Step 5: As you focus your attention on a particular person, repeat a few affirmations to yourself. These affirmations should be full of warm and positive wishes. For instance, you can direct positive energies toward your friend by saying, "May you always be happy and healthy." If you don't know someone that well, you can thank them for the ways in which they've impacted your life. For instance, you can thank your cab driver for helping you reach your destination safely. The idea is to send positive and healing vibes into the world—which then expands your own heart.

Step 6: As you focus your attention on your ex or on anyone who has let you down, you'll likely feel a surge of emotions within you. Sit with these emotions without judging yourself. Also, remember that you don't have to rush to forgive someone if you're not ready for it. What you can do is forgive yourself for all the blame and shame you carry within. For example, instead of forgiving the other person, you can direct those energies toward yourself by saying *May I find peace and hope in my life and let go of any anger and bitterness I'm still holding on to.*

Remember to give yourself grace and patience as you do this practice. You cannot expect to feel unconditional love toward others from the beginning, especially if you're still nursing wounds from the past. Take it one step at a time, and witness your heart expanding with time. As we find ourselves connected to others in the world, we're able to cut cords with those who don't have a place in our hearts anymore. When we do this without anger or bitterness, however, we're able to cut these cords without hurting ourselves in the process.

Reconnecting With Our Loving Self

One of the most powerful ways of healing our heart chakra is by diving deeper into our own ways of loving and caring for others. When we feel betrayed by someone we love, it can be hard to get in touch with all the things that make us a good friend, lover, parent, and so on. It can also be hard to focus on our own needs at the time. The following prompts can help us reconnect with ourselves on a deeper level:

- What are my five best qualities? How do these qualities help the people in my life?
- What are the five qualities I admire most in my friends, family members, and intimate partners?
- Do I treat myself the way I would want others to treat me? If not, what can I do to treat myself better?
- What are my needs in any relationship? Are those needs met? If not, am I able to communicate my needs to those in my life?
- When do I feel most loved and cherished?
- When do I feel rejected or neglected?
- Do I feel like I'm giving way more in my life than I receive? If yes, how can I correct the imbalance?
- Are there any instances in my life where I've chosen to love, forgive, and support someone even when it was difficult for me?
- How do I usually talk to myself? Is it different from how I talk to my loved ones? If yes, why is it so?
- Have you ever experienced unconditional love in your life? How has it made you feel?

Identifying Our Primary Love Language

In order to honor our own needs in relationships, it's important to understand how we like to receive love from others. In 1992, Gary Chapman published a book called The 5 Love Languages, in which he discussed the five ways in which most people communicate their love with each other. The idea came about through his experience as a marriage counselor, where he realized that many couples had good intentions but were unable to understand what their partner truly needed from them in the relationship. We can use this exercise to become more aware of our expectations in romantic relationships. Even if we don't feel ready to start dating just yet, this awareness can help us advocate for ourselves—and also prevent us from settling for less—in future relationships.

The five love languages are as follows:

- **Receiving gifts:** Do you like receiving gifts on a regular basis? These gifts don't have to be costly, but they should show you that your partner cares for you. You might even like to give thoughtful gifts to others to show your appreciation for them.
- **Quality time:** Do you enjoy spending quality time with your loved ones? Do you find shared experiences much more valuable than anything else in your relationships? Do you frequently go out of your way to spend more time with your partner or friends?
- **Acts of service:** Do you appreciate it when someone helps you or makes life easy for you in some way? This could be in the form of gifts that are utilitarian products, helping you in practical matters, or taking care of you in tangible ways. For you, actions matter much more than words.
- **Physical touch:** Do you feel loved and appreciated through displays of physical affection, including hugs, cuddles, and sex? Does your partner's touch reassure you and make you feel safe?
- **Words of affirmation:** Do you like to be appreciated through compliments, kind words, and affirmations?

One thing to understand is that we usually receive love through more than one love language. For example, I might enjoy both quality time and words of affirmation in my relationships, but I would vastly prefer spending quality time with my partner over anything else. Therefore, you should make a priority list of your love languages to understand which ones affect you the most. Also, one way to determine your love language is to observe how you give love to others. For instance, if you like complimenting people a lot, it's possible that you would like to be treated the same way by your loved ones.

Once you've made your list, you should write down the specific actions related to each relevant love language that you appreciate. If your primary love language is "quality time," you might want to go on a special date with your partner at least once a week. If you feel like you're asking for too much, gently reject the idea by telling yourself that you deserve to feel cherished in your relationship. You should also understand the difference between healthy displays of affection and neediness. For instance, it's perfectly all right to expect your partner to give you thoughtful gifts on special occasions and as surprises, but you cannot expect them to spend lavishly on you all the time. Doing this exercise will also make it easier for you to identify your future partner's love language and make them feel special in ways that they will appreciate.

Affirmations for Heart Chakra Healing

Here are some affirmations that can help us heal our heart chakra and rebuild our capacity for love and compassion:

- *I deserve love—from myself and from others.*
- *I am worthy of love at all times, and I don't need to be perfect to deserve love.*
- *I believe that love is an infinite resource whose value lies in being given and received freely.*
- *I let go of toxic attachments and welcome unconditional love into my life.*
- *I am grateful for the blessings I've received and also for the lessons I've learned in my relationships.*
- *I forgive myself for letting myself down and for sometimes abandoning myself.*
- *I let go of the pain, trauma, and anger of previous relationships.*
- *My heart is hopeful, open, and connected to the world at all times.*
- *I trust the universe to always connect me to love and abundance.*

- *I choose to embrace myself fully and to love myself for who I truly am.*
- *I choose to honor my emotions and my humanity.*
- *I am a sacred and divine being, and I choose to treat myself that way each day.*

Tools, Techniques, and Rituals for Heart Chakra Healing

Our heart chakra is related to the element of air and is represented by the color green (or pink, in some cases). Let's discuss certain rituals and techniques that can help us balance our heart chakra.

Heart Chakra Visualization

To heal your heart chakra, you can sit comfortably with your spine straight. Then, you can visualize a green or pink light emanating from your heart chakra. As you exhale, allow all the pain and resentment you've been holding on leave your being. As you inhale, allow that green or pink light to flood your heart with unconditional love.

Love Letter to Yourself

Write a letter to yourself as you would to a friend or lover. Be kind, compassionate, and supportive. Talk about your good qualities, achievements, and progress on this journey. Be appreciative of the fact that you've overcome multiple challenges in your life so far. Forgive yourself for your past mistakes and for all the times you've given up on yourself or stayed in a toxic situation for too long. Tell yourself that you deserve all the love and kindness in this world. Give this letter to a trusted friend who can give it to you after some time. Or schedule an email containing this letter to yourself in the future.

Yoga Poses for Heart Chakra Healing

In order to heal the heart chakra, we can practice asanas that can expand and strengthen our chest and shoulders. Some of the most effective asanas for this are *garudasana* (eagle pose), *ustrasana* (camel pose), *matsyasana* (fish pose), *urdhva mukha svanasana* (upward-facing dog pose), *marjaryasana* (cat pose), and *bhujangasana* (cobra pose).

YOGA POSES FOR HEART CHAKRA HEALING

Yoga Poses for Heart Chakra Healing

Some of the most effective asanas for this are garudasana (eagle pose), ustrasana (camel pose), matsyasana (fish pose), urdhva mukha svanasana (upward-facing dog pose), marjaryasana (cat pose), and bhujangasana (cobra pose).

Healing Through Crystals

One of the most powerful crystals for healing the heart chakra is rose quartz—also known as the "stone of love"—for its healing properties. It can help promote forgiveness and compassion within us. Green aventurine is another crystal that can help release emotional blockages, regulate high blood pressure, and help with heart palpitations. Green jade is a crystal that can help release negative emotions and balance our mind, body, and spirit. Other crystals that can help heal the heart chakra are rhodonite, emerald, green calcite, malachite, green opal, green tourmaline, and pink tourmaline.

Healing Through Essential Oils

Some of the best essential oils for healing the heart chakra are lavender, jasmine, cypress, geranium, rose, sandalwood, ylang-ylang, sweet orange, tangerine, mandarin, and neroli.

Journal Prompts to Help You on Your Heart Chakra Healing Journey

Here are a few prompts that can help you on your heart chakra healing journey:

- What are some instances where you've trusted someone deeply, and they've betrayed you, and how have you overcome the betrayal?
- What lessons have you learned from the most difficult relationships in your life?
- What are some limiting beliefs you have about love, and how can you overcome them?
- What do you require in a loving relationship, and are you able to communicate these needs to the people you love?
- What are some things you find difficult to forgive yourself for?
- How can you love yourself a little each day?

- How can you take care of yourself and be a good partner to yourself on a regular basis?
- How would you like to be treated by a future partner? Do you treat yourself in that manner currently?
- What is something you're still grieving, and how can you finally let it go?
- What are the little things that expand your heart throughout the day? Can you make time for these things in your regular schedule?
- What is the one kind thing you can do today—for yourself and for someone else?

Now that we've reconnected with love by healing our heart chakra, let's claim our inner truth through throat chakra healing.

Chapter 5:

Throat Chakra Healing— Finding Your Voice After Narcissistic Abuse

Happiness and freedom begin with a clear understanding of one principle: Some things are within our control, and some things are not. –Epictetus

The fifth chakra in our subtle body is known as vishuddha, or throat chakra. It's located in the pit of our throat. Physically, this chakra affects our throat, cheeks, jaw, lips, ears, shoulders, and the lower part of our neck. The throat chakra is the seat of authentic self-expression. It's associated with clarity, confidence, and communication.

When this chakra is aligned, it allows us to own our truth. We're able to speak passionately, honestly, and fearlessly. We know the value of our speech as well as our silence. Not only do we communicate with confidence and clarity, but we also allow others to express their truth in front of us. Needless to say, we can only truly be authentic when we are secure in ourselves. We know that we don't need to suppress other people's voices for our own voices to matter.

When our throat chakra is out of balance, we might suffer from various physical ailments, such as sinus infections, ear infections, sore throat, thyroid issues, gum diseases, pain and tightness in the jaw, sores in the tongue or mouth, and stiffness in the shoulders. Emotionally, a blocked throat chakra keeps us from communicating clearly and authentically. For some, it could manifest as an intense fear of speaking in public, while for others, it could mean that they don't express their needs in a relationship. The interesting thing here is that—even though speech like this seems to disgrace people other than ourselves—it also acts as a signal for how we're disregarding our own needs and insecurities.

Why does it get so difficult for us to own our truth, and how does a balanced throat chakra help us on our journey of self-expression? The quote at the beginning of this chapter talks about the sense of control that we like to have over our lives. In an ideal world, we would only have to interact with people who see us for who we truly are and embrace us wholeheartedly. Unfortunately, we meet many people in our lives who either don't give us the space to be ourselves or who actively try to sabotage our attempts at living an authentic and happy life.

Those of us who have been through an abusive relationship often know how tricky and even dangerous it can be to express ourselves in the relationship. Not only that, but we might also have communicated our needs to our ex every now and then, only to be shot down or even gaslighted by them. We might not have experienced a single honest apology or even a heartfelt conversation throughout the course of our previous relationship. What I'm trying to say is—the sanctity of speech and the beauty of authentic self-expression often get eroded in an abusive relationship. It isn't that we don't value authenticity but that we cannot believe in it any longer.

A major aspect of healing from narcissistic (and many other kinds of) abuse is accepting that we cannot change our partner's behavior, try as we might. What this also means is that we cannot keep rejecting our own truth just to appease someone who doesn't value them anyway. Even after we've left such a relationship behind, it can take us some time to live our lives the way we truly want to. Interestingly, the throat chakra is deeply related to the sacral chakra. The sacral chakra is often called the "seat of the self"—as it is related to creativity and self-expression. Think of it this way. When our sacral chakra is aligned, it allows us to tap into our creativity and emotions. When our throat chakra is aligned, it provides a voice to our creativity. In other words, the "self" finds expression through the throat chakra.

Before you learn how to reclaim your voice, consider answering a few questions to determine whether your throat chakra is out of balance:

- Do I have trouble speaking clearly, consistently, and confidently in both personal and professional scenarios?
- Do I often resort to lies, gossip, or insults in my interactions with others?
- If I were to have a conversation with myself, would I have difficulty understanding my true needs and concerns?
- Do I often feel like "swallowing my words," "biting my tongue," or "inhaling deeply" to keep my frustration in check?
- Do I worry too little about my audience? In other words, do I speak carelessly and insensitively at times—not paying enough attention to the effect my words have on others?
- Alternatively, do I worry too much about my audience? Do I feel paralyzed by fear or uncertainty to the point that I don't express myself at all?
- Do I make decisions in my life solely—or majorly—based on how others would perceive them?
- Do I feel like I'm living a life that has been designed or dictated by someone else?
- Do I feel insecure or triggered when someone around me "follows their heart" or lives an "authentic" life?
- Do I choose silence instead of honest communication in certain situations in order to protect myself?
- Do I allow others in my life to express themselves freely?
- Am I able to provide a safe space for people to be their true selves with me?

If the answer to more than half of these questions is "yes," then your throat chakra might be out of balance.

Rediscovering Self-Worth Beyond People-Pleasing

Bethany wasn't sure about the exact origins of her people-pleasing tendencies. Like many other characteristics of hers, these could have started off as self-preservation techniques—especially because she grew up in a conflict-riddled home. She often witnessed her parents fighting with each other—either using her as a shield or treating her as collateral damage in their arguments. Not only that—but when her parents' anger subsided—it often turned into icy ignorance of each other and her. Over time, Bethany began to detest the feeling that came with the "silent treatment" or the aftermath of an argument. When she grew a bit older, she learned to find ways to appease her parents in order to keep the peace. She didn't even realize when this habit of hers became an intrinsic part of her personality.

That is until she saw these patterns being played out in almost all her relationships. She would ignore her own needs in relationships, give up things that were important to her just to make things "easier" for her partner, and essentially forget herself when she was with a partner. Things came to a head in her last relationship when her people-pleasing tendencies clashed with her partner's narcissistic behavior. When she realized that, no matter what she did, she could not make her partner happy—it was as if a light had been switched on in her mind. It was the first time she considered that she couldn't force someone to love and respect her.

As she slowly started healing herself from years of abuse, she also came to terms with the fact that she had neglected herself throughout her life. Even though this neglect was a reflection of the neglect she had received in her childhood and in some of her relationships, it was now harming her instead of protecting her. Through a lot of inner work, Bethany began to understand that she didn't need approval from anyone. In fact, she couldn't guarantee their approval even if she "did everything right." The only thing left for her, then, was to figure out who she truly was and hope that people who resonated with her were able to find her. She knew that her people-pleasing tendencies were an act of self-preservation, but they had left her with almost no real sense of self. Her path to authenticity, on the other hand, would be full of challenges and would require a lot of courage—but it would also be its own reward. She knew then that she was finally ready to come out of hiding and embrace her true self.

Throat Chakra Healing

In this section, we'll discuss all about healing our throat chakra and reconnecting with our own truth.

Reclaiming Your Voice After Narcissistic Abuse

People who have been in a relationship with a narcissist often lose their voice without even realizing it. This is because abuse of any kind can be extremely insidious. It starts with something very small—almost negligible—and then snowballs into something deeply damaging and even dangerous. Therefore, you might have trouble remembering the first time you were silenced or insulted, but you know you can't express yourself confidently anymore. You might not remember all the times when your partner undermined you, but you do realize that you have difficulty trusting your own words.

While it can be painful, it's important that you spend some time thinking about some of the ways that your ex stole your voice. Only when you know how your voice was stolen will you be able to reclaim it over time. Here are a few questions you can ask yourself:

- What is an instance where my ex kept me from expressing myself?
- What are some of the times in the past when my ex insulted or ridiculed me?
- Were there instances where my ex put on a facade in front of others, making it difficult for them to believe me over him?
- Is there something negative about myself that I started believing after getting into a relationship with my narcissistic ex?
- What were some of the most common excuses that my ex made when I tried to confront them?
- Were there any lies that my ex told me?
- What is something good about myself that I still have trouble believing in because of how my ex treated me?

You can, of course, add more such questions to the list. Some of these questions will likely trigger you, so make sure that you're in a safe space and preferably around someone you trust when you do this exercise. You also don't need to complete this exercise in one sitting. If things get too intense, you should take a break and return to the exercise when you feel more centered. At the same time, I urge you to spend some time with each question and, if possible, write down your answers in as much detail as possible.

The aim of the exercise is to help us understand the extent of the damage that our ex inflicted on us. When we can focus on the seemingly isolated incidents that together served to chip away at our sense of self, we'll be able to trace them back to a voice that is not ours. Often, we cannot reclaim our voice because we cannot identify it or distinguish it from the voice of our abuser. This exercise will help us highlight this crucial difference.

Once you've identified some of the ways in which your ex robbed you of your voice, make a list of some of the recurrent fears you have about expressing yourself. Here are a few that might resonate with you:

- I feel like no one wants to listen to what I have to say.
- I don't want to be judged by others.
- I don't feel like people will believe me.
- I don't want to be misinterpreted or misunderstood by people, especially my loved ones.
- I feel safest when I don't say anything, as I feel like my words can be weaponized against me.

As you list your fears, you can also add one instance where your ex made you feel this way. For example, you can write about a time when you said something to your ex, and they used those words to make you feel guilty or ashamed. Again, it's important to remind yourself where and how these fears have originated or exacerbated due to narcissistic abuse.

After you're comfortable with this exercise, it should be easier for you to recognize your own voice as opposed to that of your "inner critic," who is often a composite of the many negative voices you've heard throughout your life. By simply becoming aware of your inner critic, you rob it of at least some of its power.

Building an Authentic Life for Yourself

It takes a lifetime to know our own selves, and sometimes, even that isn't enough. So, I won't tell you that you can know your true self in a short span of time. What you can do is get into an intimate and trusting relationship with yourself for the rest of your life. Think of it this way. When two people decide to get into a relationship, they choose to trust each other—knowing that they won't ever understand the other person completely. They choose to be vulnerable with each other, knowing that the other person cannot know everything about them. Why not treat your relationship with yourself in the same way? You don't need to understand everything about yourself, but you can be curious, respectful, and compassionate toward yourself. You can treat each day as an opportunity to know yourself better. Here are a few questions that can help you live an authentic life:

- What are your core values? In other words, what are some values that matter to you, no matter the circumstances?
- What are some of your strengths that you want to develop in the next few years?
- What are some weaknesses that you would like to overcome in the near future?
- What are the kinds of people you want to surround yourself with? What can you do to make this possible?
- What is the one aspect of your life that feels most neglected to you, and how can you focus a little more on it?
- What aspect of yourself have you compromised on in the past, and what can you do to reclaim it in the present?
- If you have to change one behavior that you currently engage in—so that you feel at peace with yourself—what would it be?
- What do you need to do to live more authentically? Is it more support from people in your life, a career change, or a different

environment? What among these things can you start working on today?

Many of us get overwhelmed when it comes to making changes in our lives, so much so that we often stay exactly where we are. Therefore, you don't need to start making huge changes to your life today. In fact, look for the smallest thing you can change that will impact your life in a meaningful way.

Healing Through Compassion, Assertion, and Accountability

If you want to live your truth, you'll need to undo what could be years of damage done to you by your abuser. Here are a few things you can do to help yourself heal:

- **Recognize your triggers and acknowledge your trauma responses:** Years of abuse can create trauma responses within us that make us feel safe and in control of difficult situations. For instance, if your partner had a habit of yelling at you, you could get extremely triggered by a loud voice. It could either drive you into a shell, or it could make you respond in a similar manner. Often, we behave in certain ways because we need to latch onto something that tells us we are protected. Identifying these behaviors and triggers can help us understand that we're safe now and that we can let go of these "protective mechanisms" and start embracing who we truly are.

- **Take back control by owning your story:** It can be debilitating for victims of abuse to deal with the manipulation of their abuser—or the disbelief of their audience—when they try to talk about their ordeals. It can be extremely frustrating when we don't get any closure from our abuser, and instead, we're made to question our own anger and pain. Choose the people you want to share your story with, decide if they're worthy of your vulnerability, and only share as much or as little as you want. Also, if you're about to share your stories with others—preserve your own safety and comfort above everything else. Recognizing that not everyone deserves to know your story is a courageous and compassionate act. Sometimes, you might need to tell your reframed story to yourself over and over until you start believing it. That's okay. Sometimes, we have to be our only audience, so make sure you're a good one.

- **Choose accountability instead of blame:** Don't get me wrong; this isn't about absolving your abuser of blame or shifting blame to yourself. What it means is recognizing what you truly have control over and using that knowledge to make your life better. What works for me is making a list of things that would make my life better and then deciding whether I have any real say in it. For instance, there are days when you might be really angry at your ex and wish that they are "punished" for their actions. It's okay to sit in those feelings for a bit and acknowledge your anger, but don't let them swallow you up. You can remind yourself that a) you might not have any real control over what happens to them, and b) their pain might not necessarily make you happier. The second point is a bitter pill to swallow for many of us and with good reason. What I can tell you—from personal experience—is that true healing happens when we focus on our own happiness rather than other people's pain. So, do for yourself what no one else did for you. Take responsibility for your emotions, your happiness, and your challenges. Be clear about what lies outside you so that you can nurture what lies within.

- **Do something you were always interested in but couldn't pursue in the past:** If you were interested in something as a child or even as an adult—and you were told that you shouldn't be wasting your time or energy over it—now's your chance to try. You don't have to be good at it or even turn it into a lifelong hobby. The important thing is to override the voices of your detractors and prove to yourself that only your voice matters.

- **Choose how you interact with people:** Another way to choose yourself is by becoming more assertive in relationships. Start small. What is the one thing you can change about your conversations with others? Would you like to be interrupted less when you're talking? Would you like others to ask what you need rather than assuming it? Are there certain behaviors that are a complete no-no for you? For instance, do you hate it when someone raises their voice at you? Remember, when you start advocating for yourself, that the other person does not have to honor your needs. However, their response to your assertion can help you understand whether you want to remain in their company in the future. Depending on what's possible, you can choose to either stop interacting with such people or at least limit your interactions with them.

- **Set boundaries with your ex:** This is for people who need to stay in contact with their abusive ex, especially if they share custody of their kids. While your ex might still try to tick you off in order to get a reaction from you, it's important to not let their voice become the noise inside your head. Once you've set your boundaries with your narcissistic ex, make sure to implement them at all times. Keep the focus on distinguishing between your voice and theirs—and your narcissistic ex will finally get the memo that they cannot control you.

- **Look for support if you need it:** When we're trying to heal ourselves from an episode of abuse, we often can't trust anyone else to understand us. While this is completely normal, it's also necessary to rebuild our trust in people and to find spaces where we can feel understood. Otherwise, we might get into a mode where we see everyone we meet as an enemy or as someone to be wary of. Also, if you're able, look for a therapist who can help you rewire your negative self-talk into a more positive narrative.

Affirmations for Throat Chakra Healing

Here are some affirmations that can help us heal our throat chakra and reclaim our voice:

- What I have to say is important and meaningful, and I deserve to be heard by others.
- I decide whom to share my story with.
- I release the pain that has been a part of my life so far.
- I release the labels forced on me by others.
- My words are healing and empowering—both for me and for others.
- I trust and honor my inner voice at all times.
- I know what I need and confidently communicate my needs in all my relationships.
- I affirm my boundaries with compassion and honesty, and I decide who can enter my space.
- I take complete accountability for my own life, and I hold others to a high standard as well.
- I own my truth and communicate with honesty at all times.
- I reject lies and manipulation in all forms.
- I communicate with kindness, courage, and respect, and deserve the same from others.
- I choose what is true to me and build my life around it.
- I honor and embrace all parts of myself with compassion and courage.
- I can only truly help others when I know who I am and what I stand for.
- This world needs me to be my authentic self.

Tools, Techniques, and Rituals for Throat Chakra Healing

The throat chakra is connected to the space element and is represented by the color blue. Here are a few techniques and rituals that can help us heal our throat chakra.

Throat Chakra Visualization

Through this exercise, we can release all the fear and pain that has kept us from expressing ourselves in an authentic manner. Sit in a comfortable position, close your eyes, and inhale deeply. As you exhale, imagine yourself releasing the pain inflicted on you by your ex, as well as the labels that have been imposed on you. As you inhale, imagine your throat filling up with a healing blue light. This light represents the courage, authenticity, and clarity you need to live the life you truly want.

Another visualization technique you can use is by imagining a set of scales. On one scale, you can place all the words and labels that have hurt you or undermined your worth. On the other scale, place all your words of affirmation and compassion. In the beginning, the scale of hurt might seem to be heavier than the healing scale. As you keep repeating the affirmations to yourself, you can imagine the two scales getting balanced—thus restoring your sense of self.

Yoga Poses for Throat Chakra Healing

Some of the most powerful poses for throat chakra healing are *bhujangasana* (cobra pose) II, *simhasana* (lion's pose), *setu bandhasana* (bridge pose), and *halasana* (plow pose).

YOGA POSES FOR THROAT CHAKRA HEALING

Yoga Poses for Throat Chakra Healing

Some of the most powerful poses for throat chakra healing are bhujangasana II (cobra pose), simhasana (lion's pose), setu bandhasana (bridge pose) and halasana (plow pose).

Healing Through Crystals

One of the most powerful crystals for throat chakra healing is aquamarine—which helps us communicate clearly and effectively and also provides the protection and courage we need to live more authentically. This is seen as a very useful crystal for those who are intensely scared of speaking in public. Another powerful crystal is the blue lace agate, which is said to help with throat-related issues and facilitate healthy self-expression. The lapis lazuli is another stone that helps promote spiritual awakening and enlightenment and enhances our communication skills and creativity. Some other crystals that can help heal the throat chakra are celestite, sodalite, amazonite, larimar, blue tourmaline, Angelite, blue topaz, blue fluorite, and blue calcite.

Healing Through Essential Oils

Some of the most effective essential oils for throat chakra alignment are jasmine, geranium, sage, frankincense, peppermint, cypress, clove, tea tree, lavender, and eucalyptus.

Journal Prompts to Help You on Your Throat Chakra Healing Journey

Here are a few prompts that can help you on your throat chakra healing journey:

- What are some labels and beliefs that I've accepted as true because of my experiences?
- How has narcissistic abuse silenced me or made me mistrust my own voice?
- What are some ways in which I've convinced myself to stay "hidden?"
- How do I feel better when accepting my truth and I am not worrying too much about how others perceive me?
- Are there any ways in which I talk to my authentic self? How can I make this conversation a regular part of my life?

- What are some challenges I face when trying to advocate for myself and my needs?
- What happens when I try to assert myself, or how do I feel when setting boundaries with others?
- When do I feel most empowered, and how can I bring that energy to all aspects of my life?
- How can I create a space where I feel safe enough to express my truth?
- What are some consequences I might have to face when I start respecting my boundaries? How can I ensure that those consequences don't compromise my safety?
- What are some things that are always true for me, and how can I ensure that I keep these aspects of me intact as much as possible?
- How can I distinguish between the voice of my abuser or other detractors from my authentic and compassionate voice?
- What are some activities that can help me express myself freely and courageously?
- What do I need to be able to express myself authentically in most, if not all, aspects of my life?

Now that we've claimed our inner truth through throat chakra healing, let's learn how to honor our intuition through third eye chakra healing.

Chapter 6:

Awakening the Third Eye— Navigating Narcissistic Abuse with Wisdom and Discernment

The first rule is to keep an untroubled spirit. The second is to look things in the face and know them for what they are. —Marcus Aurelius

The sixth chakra in our body is the third eye or ajna chakra. The word ajna means "to perceive" or "to command." This is the seat of intuition, insight, and extrasensory perception. Just as our physical eyes allow us to see the physical world with clarity, the third eye is said to be connected to the spiritual world—offering us a glimpse into the world that we often cannot sense as material beings. On the subtle body, this chakra is located exactly in the middle of our eyebrows and is connected to the pineal gland.

The pineal gland secretes the hormone melatonin—which regulates our sleep-wake cycles and biological clock through circadian rhythms. In humans, the secretion of melatonin is related to the quality of sleep and, hence, also our moods and cognitive abilities. On a spiritual level, this chakra is believed to rule the dream realm and control the veil between this world and the spirit world. When this chakra is in balance, we experience much higher levels of intuition and awareness.

Highly intuitive people are deeply connected both to themselves and the world around them. Therefore, they are able to tap into energies within and outside them. They are also able to see things and people for what they are, thus being able to make the right decisions for themselves. A balanced third eye chakra helps us in multiple ways. With greater awareness, we gain perspective around situations and people. We can see things more holistically rather than being stuck in our old patterns. New ways of seeing also mean that we become more empathetic toward others, and we're able to embrace different ways of living and being.

Most importantly, a balanced third eye chakra keeps us away from the victim mentality. In this state, we are able to acknowledge the ways in which we were wronged by our ex without giving in to helplessness or anger. Instead, we use the awareness we have to make our own lives better and break free of our own unhealthy or unhelpful patterns. Slowly, we can use the insights we receive to attract the right people into our lives. In a way, it helps us move away from bitterness and loneliness by encouraging us to make meaningful connections with others.

When this chakra is out of alignment, we feel like we cannot access our own intuition and imagination. We have difficulty receiving insights that help us solve problems, and we also have difficulty seeing the "big picture." When we aren't able to do this, it manifests as irritation and often extreme anger. There are a few ways that a blocked third eye chakra affects us. For some of us, it means that we become overly reliant on our "intellect" or logic. We don't honor our instincts, which means that we need solid evidence of each and every thing in our lives. Not only is this not possible, but it can make for a very frustrating existence.

For others, the problem could be that this chakra is "too open," which means they have difficulty staying connected to the material realm. It could lead to hallucinations and delusions—meaning we see and feel things that aren't really there. For those of us who have been victims of gaslighting in our previous relationships, this can be an especially unsettling experience—undoing weeks of healing and progress. Therefore, a major challenge for some people is to be able to stay grounded in the physical world even as their awareness opens up.

Physically and cognitively, an unbalanced third eye chakra can manifest as poor vision, headaches, ear issues, and certain neurological disorders. For people who already suffer from mental health issues, both a blocked and an overactive third eye chakra can further exacerbate their problems. It's, therefore, vital to consult a doctor or therapist before and during these sessions, just so you know that you can participate in them without any concerns.

Here are a few ways by which you can understand if your third eye chakra is balanced or not:

- Do I usually dismiss or ignore what my gut instinct is telling me at any given moment?
- Do I let others lead me when it comes to making decisions about my life?
- Do I find myself stuck in the smaller details of situations and have difficulty looking at the big picture?
- Do I feel frustrated and angry when trying to figure out the world around me?
- Do I feel depressed or hopeless about the state of the world?
- Do I have difficulty tapping into my intuition when it comes to assessing people or situations?
- Have I become more cynical or judgmental as a person?
- Do I view people and situations with mistrust or wariness?
- Do I often repeat similar behavioral patterns or attract the same kind of people in my life?
- Do I have difficulty tuning in to my inner voice in different scenarios?

If you've answered yes to more than half of these questions, your third eye chakra might be out of alignment.

Nurturing Intuition for Empowered Connections

It has been a year since Veronica left her narcissistic ex behind and started rebuilding her life, and she is very proud of the progress she has made in that time. She has also moved on from other people and relationships that don't serve her anymore. However, when it comes to making new connections, she still finds herself being hesitant. She participates in many activities in her new community and meets a lot of interesting people as well. Still, she keeps herself from knowing them too deeply or becoming too close to any of them. She has always felt safe due to this distance she has created between herself and the world, but recently, she has found herself craving authentic connections in her life.

The thing is, years of narcissistic abuse by her ex had left Veronica shaken and unsure of herself. Her ex resorted to gaslighting whenever she tried to bring up her concerns with him or when she tried to assert herself in the relationship. Slowly, his abusive tactics began chipping away at her sense of self, and they also made her question reality itself. She had difficulty distinguishing between what she wanted and what was being incessantly imposed on her. Even after she was able to leave the abusive relationship behind, it took her a long time to start believing in herself again.

Now, she feels courageous enough to live life on her own terms, but every time she feels a connection to someone else—romantic or platonic—a wave of fear and uncertainty washes over her. This is because her previous experiences have convinced her that she isn't in touch with her inner voice, or that her intuitive sense is broken forever—which makes her scared of taking chances with other people. This, of course, is not true.

The first thing Veronica needs to learn is that her intuition is neither lost nor "broken." It has simply been suppressed over the years and needs some time before it can communicate with her again. Slowly, Veronica learns to give herself time, grace, and kindness—things that she wasn't given in many of her previous relationships. As she continues her healing journey, she learns something invaluable about strengthening her intuition. She realizes that she cannot run away from mistakes if she wants to truly understand herself. Without the shame and guilt that surrounded her in her previous relationships, these mistakes will only help her get closer to her inner voice and help her distinguish the real from the unreal. By establishing firm boundaries with the people in her life, she has already taken a huge step toward honoring her intuition. Now, she needs to step out of her comfort zone and allow people to show her who they truly are—all the while loving and believing in herself.

Third Eye Chakra Healing

Before we discuss techniques for healing our third eye chakra, we need to understand something about third eye chakra alignment. Unlike most of the chakras we've discussed until now, the third eye chakra is "blocked" for many people. There could be different degrees to this "blocked" state, but many people are unable to access their intuition in a consistent manner. The more entrenched we become in the world outside us, the more alien our inner world becomes to us. At the same time, we also get a glimpse of what it means to be connected to the "reality" of this world every now and then. For example, when we experience déjà vu—we feel like we've been in the exact same situation as we are currently in, even if we know it to be impossible. Similarly, many of us have moments when we simply "know" something without being able to pinpoint the reasons for it. In this section, we will work on getting in touch with our intuition intentionally so that we have more control over how we use it to our benefit.

Another thing to keep in mind during the third eye chakra healing journey is that we need a balanced heart chakra for it. In general, it's almost impossible to access healing for higher chakras until the lower chakras are aligned. That being said, chakra balancing is neither a linear nor a one-time process. This means that we need to continuously work on making sure that our chakras are aligned. It also means that we might heal a higher chakra, but something might happen to throw a lower chakra out of balance. Sometimes, the chakra healing journey itself can cause challenges for us. What do I mean by this?

When our third eye chakra is aligned, we're able to look beyond the illusions of this world and see it for what it is. This is a boon in multiple ways, but it can also cause challenges for us. This is because many people who can see the world and its people for what it truly is end up feeling detached or depressed at its state. Some might even experience a deep state of pointlessness after recognizing this world as maya (illusion). Even on the material plane, if you're able to recognize both the good and bad in this world, how can you ensure that you keep your focus on the positive aspects? This is where we need to ensure that our heart chakra is aligned so that we aren't blocked by grief and can joyfully participate in this world. With this understanding, let's look at some of the exercises that can help us strengthen our intuition.

Getting in Touch With Your Intuition by Countering Resistance

As we saw in Veronica's case, it takes us a while to realize that we don't lose or discover our intuitive sense. Each of us has an "inner voice," which either gets strengthened or diminished as we experience more of life. For some of us, this happens when we are children. If the adults we trust dismiss our intuitive responses, we begin to believe that we don't have the capacity to see things for what they truly are. Similarly, those of us who have experienced narcissistic abuse have been repeatedly told that we're wrong and that it's our fault, even when we know that it isn't. We've been blamed for things we didn't do, words we did not utter, intentions we did not have, and decisions we did not make. No wonder, then, that we've become disconnected from our own intuitive voice.

Think of it this way. Your inner voice has been subdued by other voices—those that we can call "noise." In order to reach your voice, you need to clear this noise from within you. Here are a few ways in which you can do that:

- Take part in a detox: There are many ways in which you can purge this "noise" from your life. For one, setting healthy boundaries can ensure that you don't allow people and situations in that don't nurture you. Also, distance yourself from social media and digital media consumption for some time. This will ensure that you don't get influenced by the narratives that are presented to you on a regular basis. Last but not least, try to stay away from activities that overstimulate you.

The aim is to create a space within yourself where the "programming" of the outside world doesn't reach you.

- Let your analytical processes take a backseat: When we get into a pattern of overthinking and overanalyzing situations, we lose touch with our intuitive sense. Now, there are certain situations that certainly need proper analysis, so I'm not suggesting that you become nonchalant in all your decisions. However, if you have a habit of analyzing everything to the point of not being able to make a decision, try to let your intuition take the lead every now and then. The thing is, if we're comfortable enough to allow time and space between our analysis of a situation and the decision we make, we might allow our intuition to have a say in those decisions. Honing our intuitive sense requires, in many ways, letting go of what we think we know in order to access what we truly know.

- Get in touch with your physical self: While our cognitive processes originate in our mind, our intuition is deeply connected to our body. When we're "too much in our head," we have difficulty paying attention to how our body responds to certain people and situations. Being stuck in our mind is also often a trauma response that arises from not being able to make decisions—either because we dread the consequences of said decision or because we've been primed to think that we're no good at making decisions for ourselves. One of the best ways to access the information stored in our body is by conducting regular body scans (discussed in detail in Chapter 1). Another way to do this is by indulging in mindful movement. This could be through dance, yoga, or even walking. The aim is to let your body take over, feel safe in accessing the emotions that come up during these exercises, and use these exercises to anchor you to the present moment.

Strengthening Your Intuition Through Mindfulness, Play, and Reflection

Here are a few exercises that can help you strengthen your intuition over time.

Practice Mindfulness in Every Aspect of Your Life

We have difficulty accessing our intuition when we're too bogged down by our past experiences or too worried about the future. While some forms of advanced intuition—such as clairvoyance—can extend into the future, they still need us to be deeply and calmly connected to the world at present. This is where mindfulness comes into play. Mindfulness is a way of life, but in the beginning, it can be a major change for people who are not used to it. Therefore, be patient as you learn to become more mindful in each aspect of your life.

There are two main techniques that we'll be discussing here—mindful breathing and reflective journaling. While meditation, in general, can be a very powerful way of tapping into our intuition—by connecting us to our innermost thoughts and feelings—it can be a challenging exercise for beginners. Instead of focusing on one particular thought or feeling, we can do mindfulness meditation—in which we allow multiple thoughts and feelings to come up to the surface and observe them without letting them overwhelm us. Mindfulness meditation allows us to acknowledge whatever feelings we have and to take a step back and understand where they come from.

You can combine mindfulness meditation with reflective journaling, or you can practice reflective journaling on its own. You can write down the thoughts and feelings that arise within you, either during the mindfulness session or throughout the day, and reflect on them after a while. You can also assess certain situations and people and write down what you feel about them. It will take some time for judgment to be replaced with curiosity and detachment, but keep at it. Another thing to keep in mind when you do this exercise is that you shouldn't make your observations when you're already experiencing strong emotions.

For example, if you're already angry or elated, give yourself some time before you tap into your feelings about a person or situation.

When you revisit your observations at a later date, see if your intuition has been corroborated by later events and behaviors. Reflective journaling is also helpful for those of us who struggle to move on from the past. In the past, we've usually been told by our narcissistic partner that we're wrong about most, if not all, things. If you find yourself struggling to leave the past behind, choose to focus on instances where your ex questioned your decision-making skills and intuition. Then, think about all the realizations you've had after leaving your relationship that reinforce your faith in your intuition.

For example, if your ex had a habit of not sticking to their commitments and accused you of lying when you reminded them of the same, try to think of instances when you were proven right. You have the advantage of both time and distance from the incidents, so you can remember them with greater clarity and fewer chances of getting triggered. Each time you start to doubt yourself, remind yourself of the times in the past when you were right.

Mindful breathing is a great way to combine the benefits of meditation and breathwork and is extremely useful for those who struggle to inhabit their bodies. A great technique to calm yourself down and become rooted in the present is the "4-7-8 breathing" method. In this method, you first exhale so that your lungs are emptied of air, and then slowly inhale through the nose for four counts or four seconds. As you inhale, allow your senses to be grounded. Allow yourself to be connected to nature and the balance between stillness and movement. Then, hold your breath for seven counts and allow yourself to acknowledge those feelings that make you uncomfortable. Anything that makes you feel disconnected from your own intuition does not serve you anymore, and it needs to be expelled from your energetic body. In the last stage, you need to exhale through your mouth for eight counts. As you do so, imagine all the negative energy leaving you and, in its place, imagine a gentle and healing light flooding your chakras. This light signifies knowledge, insight, and intuition.

Affirmations for Third Eye Chakra Healing

Here are some affirmations that can help us heal our third eye chakra and get in touch with our intuition:

- I am deeply connected to my body, and I listen to what it says to me.
- I trust my intuition and inner wisdom.
- I create boundaries that protect me and prioritize my well-being and that help me know what I truly want.
- I can manifest my dreams and visions and express myself in an authentic manner.
- I am able to see both my inner and outer worlds with utmost clarity.
- I honor my imagination as limitless and powerful.
- I am able to see beyond both lies and obvious truths.
- All the wisdom and discernment I seek in my life lies within me.
- I am able to tap into the infinite wisdom of the universe and use it to live an authentic life.
- I am free of anger, anxiety, and ego—which allows me to see things with clarity and wisdom.
- I am present and connected to this moment with grace and love.
- I listen to the language of my intuition.
- I release my past and embrace my present and future potential.

Tools, Techniques, and Rituals for Third Eye Chakra Healing

The third eye chakra is connected to the "light" element and is represented by the color indigo (and, in some cases, violet). Here are a few techniques and rituals that can help us heal our third eye chakra.

Third Eye Chakra Visualization

There are many visualization and meditation practices that can help heal our third eye chakra. The first practice can be done by sitting comfortably with our spine straight and closing our eyes. As we exhale, we allow all the doubts we've harbored within us to leave our body, mind, and spirit. As we inhale, we can visualize an indigo light flooding our third eye chakra and connecting us to the wisdom and intuition of the universe.

Another form of third eye chakra visualization is known as trataka dhyana (gazing meditation). Usually, this practice is done by fixing our gaze on a candle. This practice is said to strengthen our intuition by utilizing the mind-eye connection. Before we discuss how to do this exercise, it's vital to note that children and adults with pre-existing eye conditions should not do it. Here are the steps you can follow while doing this visualization:

- Choose a slightly dark room for this exercise.
- Take a candle, light it, and place it at least 1.5 feet from where you'll be seated.
- Place the candle at eye level and sit down comfortably on a mat.
- Set an intention for this exercise.
- Close your eyes and, as you open them, direct them to the tip of the flame.
- Look at the flame for as long as you can without blinking. Your eyes will likely water a bit as you look at the flame, which is fine, but make sure you don't strain them.
- Once you feel that you cannot hold the gaze anymore, close your eyes.
- Now, visualize the flame between your eyebrows at the exact point where your third eye chakra lies.
- Keep your awareness on the flame for as long as you can until it disappears.
- Repeat this process for at least 5–10 minutes, and preferably up to 20 minutes.

This practice should ideally be done early in the morning, after your yoga practice. If you cannot get up early in the morning, then do it before going to bed at night. Over time, this practice will increase your concentration, heal your third eye chakra, and expand your awareness.

Since the third eye chakra is closely connected to the dream realm, we can use dream journaling to heal our third eye chakra. The simplest way to do this is by keeping a dream journal close to you when you sleep. When you get up in the morning or even in the middle of the night, try to note down what you remember from your dreams. It might seem like gibberish in the beginning, or the details might seem too trivial to you. Still, try to be as vivid in your descriptions as possible. Over time, you might be able to identify certain patterns emerging from your dreams or certain clues that could help you make better decisions in your life. To make this process more impactful, you can also set an intention or ask yourself a question before you go to sleep. This can give your subconscious something specific to work with. Some people also choose to work with psychoanalysts to better interpret their dreams.

Creating A Vision Board

When our third eye chakra is aligned, it can become a powerful tool for manifestations. Similarly, learning to manifest our dreams and visions can help strengthen our intuition. The best and easiest way to start your manifestation journey is by creating a vision board for the next year or even the next few years. You can also create a vision board that is related to a single goal that you want to pursue in your life. You can be as creative as you wish with the vision board, but the trick is to be specific and vivid when describing the elements of your manifestation ritual. You can use visual aids to help your mind understand what your ideal life looks like and what you can do to reach there. When it comes to this vision board, make sure that you think not only of your material goals but also about the kind of people you want in your life. Get into a habit of creating vision boards for each year or each goal in your life, and use them to live a life that is true to you.

Yoga Poses for Third Eye Chakra Healing

The most effective yoga poses for third eye chakra healing are *ardha pincha mayurasana* (dolphin pose), *salabhasana* (locust pose), *balasana* (child pose), *prasarita padottanasana* (wide-legged forward fold), and *supta matsyendrasana* (reclined twist pose).

YOGA POSES FOR THIRD EYE CHAKRA HEALING

Yoga Poses for Third Eye Chakra Healing

The most effective yoga poses for third eye chakra healing are ardha pincha mayurasana (dolphin pose), salabhasana (locust pose), balasana (child pose), prasarita padottanasana (wide-legged forward fold), and supta matsyendrasana (reclined twist pose).

Healing Through Crystals

Amethyst is by far the most powerful crystal when it comes to third-eye chakra alignment. This stone is said to enhance our intuitive powers and psychic abilities and strengthen our connection to the spiritual world. It's also a great stone for anyone who wants to become a more powerful meditator. Another crystal that is very useful for third-eye chakra healing is fluorite, which is known to be closely connected to the pineal gland. It can help fend off any negative attacks on our energy and help us expand our awareness. Some other crystals that can help in this process are sodalite, clear quartz, labradorite, azurite, celestite, ametrine, and lapis lazuli.

Healing Through Essential Oils

Some of the best essential oils for healing the third eye chakra are laurel leaf, cypress, frankincense, juniper berry, marjoram, clary sage, rosemary, patchouli, vetiver, and sandalwood.

Journal Prompts to Help You on Your Third Eye Chakra Healing Journey

Here are a few prompts that can help you on your third eye chakra healing journey:

- What are some of my past experiences that have made me doubt myself or my intuitive abilities?
- What are some of the instances where my ex told me that I was wrong, but I wasn't? How can I use these examples to build faith in myself?
- What common concerns about my past or my future hold me back from embracing the present?
- How can I stay connected to the present, even as I learn to look beyond material notions of time and space?

- What are some things I need to do to believe in my intuition and access my wisdom?
- Have there been instances where I've ignored or dismissed my gut reaction, only to be proven right at a later point in time?
- What are some aspects of my life where I give in to overthinking or overanalyzing
- How do I learn to balance my intellect and intuition?
- How does my body react around certain people or in certain situations? How do I honor my body's signals to connect deeply with my intuitive self?
- What mistakes have I made on my journey so far, and how have these mistakes helped me learn more about myself?
- What are some distractions that I need to remove from my life so that I can access my inner voice?
- Who are the people who reinforce my faith in myself, and how can I surround myself with more people like this?
- How do I protect myself from people who take advantage of my compassion without closing myself off to all the good things this world has to offer?
- How do I break free of patterns that have determined the course of my life until now?

Now that we've accessed the wisdom and intuition of the universe, let us move on to the last stage of our journey—awakening our divine self.

Chapter 7:

Awakening the Crown Chakra—Reconnecting With the Divine Self After Narcissistic Abuse

It is through your body that you realize you are a spark of divinity. –B.K.S. Iyengar

We've now reached the culmination of our healing journey. The crown chakra—also called the sahasrara—is the seventh and final chakra in our subtle body. It lies at the top of our head, where the spine meets the skull. There are some things to understand about the crown chakra before we move forward. This chakra lies firmly in the spiritual realm, and unlike with other chakras, there's no real path that leads to crown chakra awakening. This doesn't mean that we cannot reach this state, but that it's less about the actions we take and more about the way we exist in our daily lives. What do I mean by this? Let's first understand what this chakra stands for so that we can learn how to awaken it.

The crown chakra stands for the dissolution of our ego and connection with the divine consciousness. This isn't connected to any specific religious practice. Instead, it's a spiritual concept based on the belief that our individual consciousness is like a stream that originates from the universal consciousness. Our individual consciousness helps us navigate the material world, and it has the potential to merge with the divine consciousness through the crown chakra. Similarly, our ego keeps us connected to the material world and also acts as protection against things and people that could jeopardize our sense of self.

Our ego isn't a villain; in fact, it can be very useful in many instances. For example, if we've undergone abuse and need to move on in life, our ego might keep us from accessing the memories that can trigger us.

Of course, true healing can only happen when we access, confront, and heal from these memories, but we're not always prepared for that. If, for instance, we need to take care of our children or hold down a job that offers financial security—we might need the distance from the trauma that our ego provides. At the same time, when our ego becomes too powerful, it disconnects us from our deepest, truest self. In some ways, an overinflated ego means that we over-identify with our material selves.

Those of us who have undergone narcissistic abuse know this all too well. We've likely seen firsthand how an overinflated sense of self leads our partner to engage in a whole host of behaviors—such as manipulation and gaslighting (because they cannot take accountability for their actions), criticism and judgment (because they look down on everyone except themselves), and having a constant need for approval (because they are disconnected with themselves and need validation from external sources). Narcissistic abuse also wreaks havoc on the victims long after they've moved on from the abuser, and the ego plays a part there, too. We'll discuss this aspect through Shirley's story in the next section.

In terms of crown chakra, we don't look at "blocked" and "aligned" states as much as we look at an "ego state" and a "dissolution of ego" state. This dissolution of ego happens when we no longer feel threatened by our past traumas, mistakes, and memories. No longer are we bound by fear, anger, or shame. It's not that our ego is being dismantled by force. In fact, in this state, there's no need for our ego to protect us. We feel connected not only to the divine source but also to the divinity that exists in other human beings. This is a state of transcendence, faith, and surrender. Therefore, this path—if it can be called that—is one of complete surrender to a power beyond us.

Here are a few questions to ask yourself if you're still being protected by your ego or not:

- Have I become overly skeptical in various aspects of my life?
- Do I lead with fear, anger, or guilt when taking a leap of faith in a certain area of my life?

- Do I struggle to form meaningful connections with others, mostly because I'm always trying to protect myself?
- Does my mind jump to worst-case scenarios the moment I think about stepping out of my comfort zone or following my heart?
- Do I feel the urge to control every aspect of my life and even the lives of those around me?
- Am I ignoring my spiritual pursuits in favor of material comforts?
- Have I become too attached to the people and possessions in my life?
- Do I close down when I have to confront my pain or trauma?
- Do I feel stuck in certain areas of my life?
- Do certain patterns keep repeating in my life that I'm unable to get out of?
- Am I unable to place my trust in a higher power?
- Do I struggle to find meaning and purpose in my life, even if my life is comfortable and successful in the conventional sense?

If you've answered yes to more than half of these questions, you might be overly connected to your ego.

Going Beyond the Ego and Accessing the Divine Self

The years after leaving her narcissistic ex behind were full of confusion for Shirley. On one hand, she felt liberated like never before and was eager to take control of her life. On the other hand, she was regularly reminded of how she had to submit to her ex's ego trips. When she finally left him behind, she vowed to herself that she would never let someone else have any control over her. Understandably, she went into a defensive mode each time someone tried to come close to her. She protected herself and her loved ones fiercely, to the point that she closed herself off to new people and experiences.

Another thing happened in the aftermath of the narcissistic abuse. Shirley had always been very attached to her family, but nowadays, she found herself being overly attached to them. Not only to her family but she was excessively attached to the life she had built and the identity she had created for herself. This made sense to her. She had worked so hard and overcome so much to reach this point in her life. No wonder she wanted to protect it from the outside world.

Over time, Shirley began to notice that she was unable to fully experience life. She felt like something always held her back from giving in to the joys and wonders of life. Through various mindfulness and meditation sessions, she realized that her ego had been holding down the fort for quite some time. It was protecting her from further hurt, but it was also preventing her from realizing her true spiritual potential. She understood that fear and anger had helped her stay away from people who could take advantage of her in the past, and they had ensured that she could create a safe home for her children and loved ones. However, these emotions didn't serve her anymore. She could now thank her ego for taking care of her while also acknowledging that she didn't need her ego to protect her anymore.

By acknowledging the protection of the divine consciousness in her life, she was able to acknowledge and celebrate her divine self. She was ready to accept unconditional joy and bliss into her life.

Crown Chakra Awakening

The biggest block to crown chakra awakening is "attachment." Attachment isn't a bad thing in itself. After all, we're attached to many things that make our life worth living. Even if we aren't attached to material wealth, for example, we can be attached to the idea of making life comfortable for our loved ones. Attachment isn't only about fear, anger, jealousy, and grief. In fact, the love we have for others in our life might be our biggest attachment. So, how do we move on from attachment and live a life of loving detachment?

To understand this, we need to understand what detachment truly is. Detachment isn't the same as carelessness, callousness, or lack of commitment. Detachment isn't the same as escapism; you cannot run away from your responsibilities or give up on your worldly pursuits and call yourself an awakened being. Detachment is a practice, a dance, and a commitment to joy. In fact, true detachment might enable you to engage more deeply with life. When we talk about detachment in the spiritual sense, we're talking about detachment from the outcome of our actions. If we only make choices based on their consequences—which cannot be predicted—we might never follow our true calling or live a blissful life. Worry, anxiety, and fear will keep us from doing what seems best for us.

True detachment doesn't ask us to forget the world. In fact, it asks us to forget our urge to control our world. When we do this, paradoxically, we can participate in the world in the most beautiful way possible. Here are a few steps you can take to practice mindful detachment in your life:

- Acknowledge how you feel regarding things and people: You can start with one person and try to understand what feelings arise when you think of them. For instance, you might think of your ex and notice that you get angry, sad, or defensive because of your past experiences with them. Or you can think of your child and feel the love, care, and concern that arise during that time. We cannot detach from something that we ignore or repress. Remember that we're trying to detach from the emotions and defense mechanisms that hold us back, and not necessarily from the people themselves in every case.

- Breathe into the discomfort: Ask yourself why these emotions come up when you think of something or someone. For example, if you've been meaning to start your own business for a while but cannot get over the initial inertia, ask yourself why you feel this way. Name your fears and concerns and trace them back to previous experiences. They're likely tied to something that makes you uncomfortable. Have you, for instance, tried to do something on your own and not been very successful at it in the past? Has your ex or someone else told you that you cannot do well on your own? This will not be pleasant, but it's important to focus on these instances so that we can let go of them. Practicing mindfulness can really help us focus on these emotions without getting overwhelmed by them.

- Consider the "growth value" of difficult experiences: This isn't the same as toxic positivity. You don't need to act like you deserved the pain you've gone through or that you should get over things simply because they are in the past. You can acknowledge how lonely or angry you felt at the time while also focusing on something good that came out of it. Was there a lesson you learned for the future? Did you become more independent as a result? Were you able to decenter romantic relationships from your life and focus on your spiritual growth for some time? We do this to take the "sting" away from these experiences and enter a space of gratitude and healing.

- Offer your worries to a higher power: I'm not saying that you need to relinquish your responsibilities. On the contrary, you show your commitment to meaningful detachment by having faith in a higher power. Offer your anger, love, compassion, envy, and grief to this entity. Tell yourself that you're taken care of at all times. This is the stage of surrender—where you begin to see everything as cosmic play or lila.

Affirmations for Crown Chakra Healing

Here are some affirmations that can help us awaken our crown chakra and surrender to our divine self:

- I am a divine being and a treasured part of this universe.
- My energy resonates with the cosmic energy of this universe—healing me and those around me.
- I am on the path to cosmic wisdom and self-realization.
- I can channel the universal consciousness to achieve my divine purpose.

- My past pain morphs into healing and wisdom.
- I am always connected to a higher power that guides and protects me through life.
- I deserve unconditional joy, love, and peace in my life.
- I am the embodiment of love and light.
- I release control of my life and allow my guides to show me the path that honors who I am.
- Even on the dark days, I am always connected to the source of infinite power, wisdom, and love.
- I consider my difficult experiences with curiosity and a willingness to learn from them.
- I respect my own emotions and intentions and afford the same respect to others.
- I am free from the illusion of separation from the divine.
- I have the patience and consideration to understand that others are on a journey of their own.

Tools, Techniques, and Rituals for Crown Chakra Awakening

The crown chakra is a unique chakra because it's not connected to any element. In fact, it's represented by "silence." In terms of color, while some schools of thought believe that purple or violet represents this chakra, others believe that white is the best representation of it. This is because the color white encompasses all the colors in the visible spectrum, which symbolizes that the crown chakra can incorporate all aspects of our existence. Let's discuss a few rituals that can help us awaken our crown chakra.

Since this is the final chakra on our chakra healing journey, we need to understand its significance in our material and spiritual lives. Throughout the book, we've been talking about yoga asanas that can help us balance different chakras in our bodies. This is a good place to discuss what yoga means in the original Hindu and Buddhist traditions. The word "yoga" means "to join," which signifies spiritual union with the divine. So, while yoga is often seen as a great technique for improving physical and mental wellness, its original role was to get us closer to the universal consciousness.

Therefore, when we think of yoga, we should approach it more as a spiritual exercise than a purely physical one. In the yogic traditions, the highest form of spiritual enlightenment—that occurs when the crown chakra awakens—is called samadhi. This is a state of utter bliss, and it is only achieved through the "pathless path." Since this is only possible with complete surrender, we need to think of ways of reducing our resistance to the divine energy. Often, this resistance isn't conscious, but it has a huge impact on our spiritual journey.

Crown Chakra Visualization

The crown chakra is represented by a thousand-petaled lotus. We will be using this symbol for our visualization exercise. Sit down comfortably on the floor and close your eyes. Keep your spine straight, and imagine a beautiful white thousand-petaled lotus resting on the top of your head. As you exhale deeply through your mouth, allow all your doubts, fears, and negative attachments to leave your being. On inhaling deeply through your nose, imagine a pure white light flooding your crown chakra and causing the lotus to bloom. Then, let that light enter your spine through the crown chakra and flood your entire being—helping you experience a sense of calm as you've never known before.

Another powerful crown chakra visualization is about giving up on our fears and doubts. Before doing this exercise, write down your biggest fears or doubts, as well as some of your past experiences that still cause you pain. Then, sit down as you would for any visualization exercise. Take a deep exhale and allow all the residual energy to leave your body. As you inhale through your nose, think of a future where you aren't burdened by your current fears or doubts. What will happen if you take a leap or make new friends? How will your life improve if you are able to let go of your fears? Think of these situations as if they're happening in real time. Immerse yourself in the joy and freedom you experience when you live out your soul's true purpose. When you're thinking about these scenarios, you'll likely still experience some doubts and fears every now and then. Instead of dismissing them, thank them for keeping you safe as you exhale deeply through your mouth.

When this exercise is complete, write down how you felt during your visualization. You can also include the details of the visualization exercise to make yourself feel more connected to your true purpose. Then, you can write down the steps you can take today to get closer to your truth. For example, if you want to quit your toxic job and do something that creatively enriches you, don't think about all the things that are holding you back. Instead, think about that one small step that you can take toward your dream. Is there a way for you to build your creative profile outside of work? Can you save a little more money each month to build an emergency fund for yourself? As you begin to connect your dreams to practical goals and milestones, you'll get closer to living the life you really want to live.

Spending Time in Silence

Before we talk about the crown chakra, we need to discuss the importance of bija mantras on our chakra healing journey. There are different sounds—also known as bija mantras (seed syllables)—that can help us during our chakra healing journey. These mantras are known to carry powerful vibrations of the universe, which can help align each of the six chakras (excluding the crown chakra). Here are the bija mantras that can be used for healing the six chakras:

Root chakra: LAM

Sacral Chakra: VAM

Solar Plexus Chakra: RAM

Heart Chakra: YAM

Throat Chakra: HAM

Third Eye Chakra: OM

These bija mantras work in a way that is similar to affirmations, but they are much more powerful than normal affirmations. Therefore, we should be careful while chanting these mantras and make sure that our intentions are pure and clear when we do so. You'll also notice that there is no bija mantra for crown chakra awakening, and that's because this chakra is connected to silence.

In today's world, it can be challenging to find a space where we can sit in silence. It can also be unsettling for many of us to be alone with our thoughts in silence. While meditation is a great tool to practice silence in our daily lives, we can also learn to be silent in other ways. For example, you can build a "sanctuary" for yourself at home, where you spend at least 15–20 minutes in silence every day. You can read a book during this time or even do a journaling exercise, but it would be best if you could do nothing at this time. As I said, it can be challenging to be alone with your thoughts in the beginning, but resist the urge to "do" something in order to escape this discomfort. You can try breathing deeply during this time so that your focus shifts to your breath. You can also conduct a body scan that allows you to fully connect with your emotions through your body.

Another great way to spend time in silence is through nature walks. Many of us listen to music while walking, but try to avoid doing this when on your crown chakra awakening journey. Instead, allow the sounds of nature to surround and soothe you. If you can, spend some time each week in a forest with a thick canopy. This can make you feel both safe and deeply connected to nature.

Learning the Art of Surrender

This is perhaps the most challenging thing that any human being can learn, as well as the most rewarding. Life as a human being is marked by uncertainty, and we need to make numerous decisions while making peace with the various unknowns in our lives. What's more, we might do everything right and prepare for every eventuality and still end up in a situation that we had not anticipated. For people who have undergone abuse of any kind, it can be especially challenging to trust anyone outside of themselves. It can also be difficult to believe that the universe has a plan for us when we've undergone something traumatic. It's like the spiritual equivalent of a trust fall. We cannot be expected to close our eyes and fall on our backs—trusting the universe to hold us—when we've fallen down and hurt ourselves in the past.

I'll be honest with you: You will not reach the stage of surrender overnight. Instead, you need to take one small step each day that strengthens your faith in the universe. Here are a few things you can do to enable the process:

- Think of one aspect of your life where you can loosen your grip a little: When you're still recovering from trauma, your defenses will be up, and you might want to overcontrol every aspect of your life. However, you can take small steps to overcome your controlling tendencies. Think of an area in your life where you feel the least fear and resistance. Since this is the last chakra on your healing journey, you've likely lowered your resistance in various aspects of your life. For example, you might be feeling confident about your professional life after your solar plexus chakra healing journey. Therefore, you can try to take a few risks when it comes to your job. Or you might be willing to take chances with your heart again. If you feel scared and anxious, that's okay. Allow the universe to step in and take care of things for you.

- Ask the universe for signs: This will take some time to master, but it can really help you sharpen your intuition and become more receptive to the energy of the universe. You can do this exercise before your meditation session. Set an intention for the meditation and ask the universe a question that has been on your mind for some time. Then, sit in silence and breathe deeply, indicating your willingness to "listen to" the answer. You won't always receive the answer immediately—it can take a while for that to happen—but it will come to you when the time is right.

- Respond to the universe's messages: To prove your faith in the universe, you'll need to pay attention to the messages you receive from it and act accordingly. The thing is, you might not always like what the universe offers you. What if the signals lead to something that you don't like or hadn't planned for yourself? What if the universe asks you to follow a path that isn't your first or second choice? If you feel unsure of the universe's answer, keep engaging with it in good faith. You can always ask your guides more questions and let them help you understand their plan for you. Ultimately, though, you'll have to take the plunge.

- Reframe how you see your past experiences: When we've gone through a bad experience in the past, we might be overly focused on the fact that we were dealt a bad hand by the universe. How about looking at things a bit differently? Why not remember all the times when you were held by an unknown force in your life? Why not show gratitude for the fact that you were able to leave your abusive relationship behind and start afresh? Think of all the times the universe stepped in and protected you, and you'll feel more receptive to its energy in the future—even if you don't always understand it.

Yoga Poses for Crown Chakra Awakening

The most powerful yoga poses for crown chakra awakening are padmasana (lotus pose), supta baddha konasana (reclined bound angle pose), salamba sarvangasana (supported shoulder stand), sasangasana (rabbit pose), and savasana (corpse pose).

YOGA POSES FOR CROWN CHAKRA AWAKENING

Yoga Poses for Crown Chakra Awakening

The most powerful yoga poses for crown chakra awakening are padmasana (lotus pose), supta baddha konasana (reclined bound angle pose), salamba sarvangasana (supported shoulder stand), sasangasana (rabbit pose), and savasana (corpse pose).

Awakening Through Crystals

One of the most effective crystals for crown chakra awakening is clear quartz, which can help in channeling divine wisdom. Amethyst is another crystal that can help us access higher states of consciousness. Selenite is a stone that helps us achieve spiritual clarity and awaken our crown chakra. Apart from these crystals, lepidolite, diamond, apophyllite, and labradorite are also very helpful in connecting us to the universal consciousness.

Awakening Through Essential Oils

The best essential oils for crown chakra awakening are Chinese rice flower, white lotus, jasmine, lavender, cedarwood, galbanum, rose, myrrh, neroli, and gurjum.

Journal Prompts to Help You on Your Crown Chakra Awakening Journey

Here are a few prompts that can help you on your crown chakra awakening journey:

- What are some experiences in my past that trigger me and activate my defense mechanisms?
- How can I acknowledge and honor my grief and pain while also releasing them to the universe?
- How does my ego prevent me from experiencing life to the fullest?
- What prevents me from connecting deeply to myself and those around me?
- How can I surrender to the universe without shirking my responsibilities toward myself and others?
- What would my life look like if it wasn't marked by fear, anger, or anxiety?
- How can I bring more unconditional joy and love into my life?

- What can I do to honor myself as a divine being?
- How can I prepare myself to receive the abundance of the universe?

Conclusion

Healing takes courage, and we all have courage, even if we have to dig a little to find it. –Tori Amos

When we've gone through years of narcissistic abuse, it can take us a while to find the courage we need to heal ourselves. Even after making the life-affirming decision to move away from our abuser, we have a host of challenges in front of us. Narcissistic abuse wreaks havoc on every aspect of our being. Not only that, but the energetic damage it unleashes on us can take a long time to undo. This is also why, despite all our efforts to create a new life for ourselves, some of us struggle to reach the state of peace, joy, and love that we truly deserve. I wrote this book to provide hope to anyone who envisions a better life for themselves but doesn't know how to take that first step. Through this book, we took a unique approach and focused on chakra healing to counter the negative effects of narcissistic abuse on our physical, mental, emotional, and spiritual health.

In this book, we talked about how each chakra is related to different aspects of our body, mind, and spirit. We also discussed different stories that focused on the effect that narcissistic abuse can have on our respective chakras. In each chapter, we first understood whether a particular chakra was aligned or not, and then we discussed why that chakra was out of balance. Then, we moved on to healing each chakra—through various rituals and techniques. We also focused on the power of visualizations, affirmations, and yoga to heal each chakra. In the end, we talked about using various crystals and essential oils to bring our chakras back into alignment.

Here are a few things that we've learned in this book:

- The first chapter was about healing the root chakra. As the first or lowest chakra, the root chakra is all about stability and security. We discussed ways of overcoming our fear and anxiety as we recover from narcissistic abuse, and we also learned how to connect to the earth and use its healing energy to feel more grounded in our everyday lives. Only when this chakra is aligned can we begin to work on other aspects of our lives, so this was a crucial first step on the journey.

- The second chapter helped us focus on the sacral chakra—the seat of sexuality, emotions, and creativity. In this chapter, we looked at ways that shame can come in the way of self-expression and how we can connect to the healing energy of water and reconnect with our emotions and creativity after narcissistic abuse. One major part of this healing process was learning to heal our inner child and getting in touch with aspects of ourselves that we've had to repress in the past.

- In the third chapter, we learned all about reclaiming our personal power after having to give it away to our abuser in the past. By connecting to the energy of fire, we learned how to become resilient and assertive and to move confidently through life. Like the Sun, we became both powerful and optimistic through solar plexus chakra healing.

- One of the most difficult aspects of healing from narcissistic abuse is being able to heal our hearts and open them up to new people and relationships. In the fourth chapter, we discussed how grief can block our heart chakra and make us close ourselves to the possibility of love and compassion. By connecting to the healing energy of the air element, we held space for our grief while also acknowledging that we don't need it anymore. This chakra is also the bridge between the "physical" and "spiritual" chakras, and learning to heal it made us ready for our spiritual awakening journey.

- In the fifth chapter, we channeled the energy of the space element to reclaim our lost voice after narcissistic abuse. We understood how lies and gaslighting can make us doubt our reality and forget our authentic voice. Through throat chakra healing, we learned to listen to our inner voice, silence the voice of our abusive ex or other critics, and build an authentic life for ourselves.

- The sixth chapter was all about the third-eye chakra awakening. In this chapter, we learned how narcissistic abuse can make us feel disconnected from our intuition and how we can learn to trust our gut again. We talked about the challenges we might face when trying to access the wisdom of the universe that is already within us, as well as the methods we can use to counter the resistance that arises during this process. We used the energy of light to see beyond the illusions that we encounter on a daily basis.

- In the last chapter, we reached the final milestone of our spiritual journey. At this point, we were ready to embrace the divine energy that has always been a part of us but that might have been neglected in the past. In our quest for unconditional love, joy, and peace—we begin to question the ties of toxic attachment that often hold us back from realizing our true destiny. To awaken our crown chakra, we had to let go of our fears, doubts, and our urge to control everything in our lives. We had to understand how true detachment was instrumental to the idea of Divine Union, and we often stand in our own way simply because we don't trust the universe. Learning to participate in the cosmic dance without questioning what the dance means or what the music is trying to tell us might just be the key to making our lives happier and more meaningful.

I hope that this book has helped you take your first step toward the life that you truly deserve to live. I'll leave you with this: You don't need to know everything when you start out. You can figure out your way as long as you keep moving in the right direction. In the end, true healing comes from decentering the abuse and the abuser from our lives and focusing on our own potential.

There's something about the healing process that I would like to leave you with. Healing is neither easy nor linear, and it's certainly not something that can be treated as a short-term goal. When we're subjected to trauma, loss, or abuse of any kind—it can take us an entire lifetime to come to terms with the pain and devastation that comes with it. This isn't a bad thing because healing opens us up in ways that we might have never considered before. However, it can be challenging to stay committed to this journey when things get tough, which is why

I urge you to think of it as the highest form of love. If you can hold space for yourself as you navigate one of the most difficult periods of your life, you will find your heart and soul expanding in the most beautiful way possible. You owe this to both your past and your future self.

In the end, I ask that if this book has inspired you in any way, please consider leaving a review on Amazon so that others might find it when they need it the most.

References

Amos, T. (2023, June 6). Anne Rice quotes. Southern Living.
https://www.southernliving.com/culture/healing-quotes

Anne. (2023, October 11). How to get back to yourself after
emotional abuse. Betrayal Trauma Recovery.
https://www.btr.org/how-to-get-back-to-yourself-after-
emotional-abuse/

Annette, N. C. (2022, January 21). Understanding ho'oponopono.
Metta365.
https://metta365.com/blog/understandinghooponopono

Aurelius, M. (n.d.-a). Marcus Aurelius quotes. Goodreads.
https://www.goodreads.com/quotes/190580-you-have-
power-over-your-mind---not-outside-events

Aurelius, M. (n.d.-b). Marcus Aurelius quotes. Goodreads.
https://www.goodreads.com/quotes/20870-the-first-rule-is-
to-keep-an-untroubled-spirit-the

Aurelius, M. (n.d.-c). Marcus Aurelius quotes. BrainyQuote.
https://www.brainyquote.com/quotes/marcus_aurelius_1321
63

Balancing the crown chakra with essential oils and aromatherapy.
(n.d.). AromaWeb.

https://www.aromaweb.com/essentialoilschakras/essential-oils-crown-chakra-guide-tips.php

Balancing the heart chakra with essential oils and aromatherapy. (n.d.). AromaWeb. https://www.aromaweb.com/essentialoilschakras/essential-oils-heart-chakra-guide-tips.php

Balancing the solar plexus chakra with essential oils and aromatherapy. (n.d.). AromaWeb. https://www.aromaweb.com/essentialoilschakras/essential-oils-solar-plexus-chakra-guide-tips.php

Balancing the third eye chakra with essential oils and aromatherapy. (n.d.). AromaWeb. https://www.aromaweb.com/essentialoilschakras/essential-oils-third-eye-chakra-guide-tips.php

Brooks, H. (2023, October 16). How I healed from gaslighting and found self-love after the abuse. Tiny Buddha. https://tinybuddha.com/blog/how-i-healed-from-gaslighting-and-found-self-love-after-the-abuse/

Burgin, T. (2020, December 15). Nada yoga: Union through sound. Yoga Basics. https://www.yogabasics.com/connect/yoga-blog/nada-yoga-union-through-sound/

Camille. (2023, July 13). 10 best yoga poses for the third eye chakra. Everything Yoga Retreat.

https://www.everythingyogaretreat.com/yoga-poses-third-eye-chakra/

Crown chakra crystals. (2024, January 3). Anahana. https://www.anahana.com/en/wellbeing-blog/yoga/crown-chakra-crystals

Crown chakra (Sahasrara). (2023, October 11). Anahana. https://www.anahana.com/en/yoga/crown-chakra

Dittmar, G. (2021, February 1). 3 beginner breathwork techniques & the best time of day to do them. Mindbodygreen. https://www.mindbodygreen.com/articles/breathwork-techniques-for-beginners

Doherty, J. (2023a, October 10). The crown chakra: Discover and balance the seventh chakra. Art Of Living (United States). https://www.artofliving.org/us-en/meditation/chakras/crown-chakra-seventh

Doherty, J. (2023b, October 10). The third eye chakra: Discover and balance the sixth chakra. Art Of Living (United States). https://www.artofliving.org/us-en/meditation/chakras/third-eye-chakra-sixth

Emerson, C. H. (2023, December 1). Pineal gland. Encyclopedia Britannica. https://www.britannica.com/science/pineal-gland

Epictetus. (n.d.-a). Epictetus quotes. BrainyQuote. https://www.brainyquote.com/quotes/epictetus_132944

Epictetus. (n.d.-b). Epictetus quotes. Goodreads.
https://www.goodreads.com/quotes/10517315-happiness-and-freedom-begin-with-a-clear-understanding-of-one

Everything you need to know about the heart chakra. (2021, March 11). Yoga Journal. https://www.yogajournal.com/yoga-101/chakras-yoga-for-beginners/intro-heart-chakra-anahata/

Fierce self-compassion break. (2023, November 14). Greater Good in Action.
https://ggia.berkeley.edu/practice/fierce_self_compassion_break

Franquemont, S. (2006). Exercises for developing your Intuition. Taking Charge of Your Health & Wellbeing.
https://www.takingcharge.csh.umn.edu/activities/exercises-developing-your-intuition

Heart chakra crystals - Explore love and harmony. (2024, January 3). Anahana. https://www.anahana.com/en/wellbeing-blog/yoga/heart-chakra-crystals

Iyengar, B. K. S. (n.d.). B.K.S. Iyengar quotes. Goodreads.
https://www.goodreads.com/quotes/7087-it-is-through-your-body-that-you-realize-you-are

Jain, R. (2020, September 16). Unlock the secrets of your heart chakra: The complete guide. Arhanta Yoga Ashrams.
https://www.arhantayoga.org/blog/anahata-chakra-heart-chakra-self-realization-through-love/

Jain, R. (2023, September 10). Crown Chakra: Discover the divine energy of sahasrara chakra. Arhanta Yoga Ashrams. https://www.arhantayoga.org/blog/crown-chakra-divine-energy-of-sahasrara-chakra/

Lechner, T. (2019, August 27). 5 steps to detaching for a happier life. Chopra. https://chopra.com/blogs/mind-body-health/5-steps-to-detaching-for-a-happier-life

Le Guin, U. K. (2021, September 2). Ursula K. Le Guin quotes. Linearity Blog. https://www.linearity.io/blog/creativity-quotes/

Lizzy. (2019a, December 9). 3 simple yoga poses to open your heart chakra. Chakras.info. https://www.chakras.info/heart-chakra-yoga-poses/

Lizzy. (2019b, December 24). 5 simple yoga poses to activate the solar plexus chakra. Chakras.info. https://www.chakras.info/yoga-poses-solar-plexus-chakra/

Loggins, B. (2023, December 26). Healing from narcissistic abuse. Verywell Mind. https://www.verywellmind.com/stages-of-healing-after-narcissistic-abuse-5207997#toc-tips-for-healing-from-narcissistic-abuse

McGee, J. (2023, April 12). How to reclaim your identity after narcissistic abuse. Jim McGee Coaching. https://jimmcgeecoaching.com/identity-after-narcissistic-abuse/

Mulholland, J. (2024, January 26). Success is in surrender: Four ways to let the universe help you. Plenty. https://www.plentyconsulting.com/news/success-is-in-surrender-four-ways-to-let-the-universe-help-you

Newlyn, E. (2019, November 5). How to practice trataka: Using a candle for meditation. Yogamatters. https://blog.yogamatters.com/how-to-practice-trataka-using-a-candle-for-meditation/

Nguyen, J. (2020, October 21). Why everyone's talking about love languages these days & how to find yours. Mindbodygreen. https://www.mindbodygreen.com/articles/the-5-love-languages-explained

Nunez, K. (2020, June 9). 5 benefits of metta meditation and how to do it. Healthline. https://www.healthline.com/health/metta-meditation

Rakshak. (2024, January 3). A brief introduction to tratak meditation. The Art of Living. https://www.artofliving.org/in-en/meditation/guided/tratak-meditation

Rankin, L. (2023, April 12). 18 ways to strengthen your Intuition. Mindbodygreen. https://www.mindbodygreen.com/articles/how-to-strengthen-your-intuition

Rice, A. (2020, December 1). Anne Rice quotes. Passion Writes Life. https://www.passionwriteslife.com/25-quotes-about-abuse-recovery-to-help-you-move-on/

Saeed, K. (2018, August 22). Healing from identity loss after narcissistic abuse. Psych Central. https://psychcentral.com/blog/liberation/2018/08/healing-from-identity-loss-after-narcissistic-abuse#The-Narcissists-Misunderstood-Sense-of-Self

Smith, C. (2023, December 9). 10 throat chakra yoga poses. Chakra Practice. https://chakrapractice.com/throat-chakra-yoga-poses/

Snyder, S. (2022, September 4). Everything you need to know about the throat chakra. Yoga Journal. https://www.yogajournal.com/yoga-101/chakras-yoga-for-beginners/chakratuneup2015-intro-visuddha/

Solar plexus chakra crystals - Unleashing the powers. (2023, March 7). Anahana. https://www.anahana.com/en/wellbeing-blog/yoga/solar-plexus-chakra-crystals

Third eye chakra crystals - Enhancing clarity & communication. (2024, January 3). Anahana. https://www.anahana.com/en/wellbeing-blog/yoga/third-eye-chakra-crystals

Throat Chakra Crystals - Become more creative. (2024, January 3). Anahana. https://www.anahana.com/en/wellbeing-blog/yoga/throat-chakra-crystals

Top 10 throat chakra essential oils. (n.d.). Chakra Anatomy. https://www.chakra-anatomy.com/throat-chakra-essential-oils.html

Vowell, C. (2023, September 18). Intuition training: 5 exercises to strengthen intuition. Positive Psychology. https://positivepsychology.com/intuition-training/

Your voice – What it is and how it is silenced by the narcissist. (2015, May 4). After Narcissistic Abuse. https://afternarcissisticabuse.wordpress.com/2015/05/04/your-voice-why-and-how-its-silenced-by-the-abusive-narcissist/

Image References

All images have been provided by the author.

Made in the USA
Monee, IL
17 May 2024

58584346R00074